Easy Steps to
**POWERPOINT®** 2010

*Paula L. Smith*

MINDSTIR MEDIA

*Easy Steps Learning Series: Easy Steps to PowerPoint 2010*
Copyright © 2013 by Paula L. Smith. All rights reserved.

Edited by Waitee Smith

Published by Mindstir Media
PO Box 1681 | Hampton, New Hampshire 03843 | USA
1.800.767.0531 | www.mindstirmedia.com

Printed in the United States of America

ISBN: 978-0-9892711-7-2
LCCN: 2013937356

Visit Paula L. Smith on the World Wide Web:
www.easystepslearningseries.com

Microsoft®, PowerPoint®, Microsoft Office®, Windows 7®, and Windows
Vista® are either registered trademarks or trademarks of Microsoft
Corporation in the United States and/or other countries.

Easy Steps Learning Series® and the Easy Steps Learning Series logo are
trademarks or registered trademarks of Providing Leading Solutions, LLC in
the United States and/or other countries.

Other product and names mentioned herein may be the registered trademarks
or trademarks of their respective owners.

# EASY STEPS LEARNING SERIES

## Easy Steps to PowerPoint 2010

## Table of Contents

# Acknowledgements

First, I want to thank God, who empowers me to do what I do. Thanks to all my family and friends who prayed and supported me through this endeavor. I am very grateful to develop the Easy Steps Learning Series to help someone learn or advance in their technology skills.

# About the Author

Paula has worked in the information technology industry for over 25 years. Her work ethics, honesty, integrity, high energy and ability to communicate at any corporate or non-corporate level makes her one of the strongest information technology leaders in the industry today.

Paula has expertise in diverse range of technologies within multiple industry settings. She has demonstrated success in Training, Project Management, Software Design, Quality Assurance, Product Development, Network Operations, and Internet and e-Commerce Technology.

Paula is the CEO of Providing Leading Solutions, LLC, author of the Easy Steps Learning Series©, PMO Project Manager, Microsoft Partner, Microsoft Certified Trainer, Microsoft Certified Information Technology Professional, Microsoft Certified Technology Specialist, Microsoft Office Master Instructor, Microsoft Office Master, Microsoft Office Expert, Microsoft Office Specialist. She holds over several Microsoft Certifications, Train-The-Trainer Certification and has been Microsoft beta tester for many Microsoft products.

She is a member of the Microsoft Office Community, Microsoft Office Live Small Business, Microsoft TechNet, Project Management Institute, Enterprise Project Management, and Microsoft Project User Groups. Paula enjoys the arts, cooking, song writing, geek gadgets, and technology.

# EASY STEPS LEARNING SERIES

Easy Steps to PowerPoint 2010

# Introduction

The purpose of this book is to provide easy steps, interactive practical exercises and review questions or answers to learn Microsoft PowerPoint 2010 application. This book is for the novice, intermediate or advance user. You may want to learn more about PowerPoint to advance your skills or simply become a Microsoft Office Specialist in PowerPoint 2010; this is the right book for you.

Easy Steps Learning Series takes a more simplistic approach with step by step interactive learning methods. There are interactive practice exercises, review questions and answers to reinforce your learning journey. This book provides a more time-saving learning method of a visual and kinestatic approach.

The history of PowerPoint is a true story of triumph and persistence. The brain child of the PowerPoint product was Robert Gaskins and Dennis Austin. They formed a company called Forethought and submitted a sample product proposal for a presentation graphics for overhead projection to the company, Apple.[1]

Apple was a strategic venture capitalist for the product. The original name was **"Presentation"** and changed to **"PowerPoint"** because of trademark issues. The first PowerPoint 1.0 for Mac was created in 1987.[2]

---

[1] Gaskins, Robert. 2012. *Sweating Bullets: Notes about Inventing PowerPoint.* San Francisco and London: Vinland Books, 512 pp. ISBN (paperback) 978-0-9851424-2-1. Library of Congress Control Number 2012936438. 20 April 2012. Archived searchable full text with hyperlinks at www.robertgaskins.com/powerpoint-history/sweating-bullets/gaskins-sweating-bullets-webpdf-isbn-9780985142414.pdf

[2] Ibid.

Microsoft later made the acquisition of the product and created the Microsoft Graphics Business Unit. It was headed by Robert Gaskins in 1992.[3]

What a phenomenal breakthrough in software applications for Mac and Windows. PowerPoint presentations are used in about every industry corporately and widely used by numerous churches and religious institutions. There are approximate around 500 million PowerPoint users today worldwide.[4]

---

[3] Ibid.

[4] Gaskins, Robert, *Resume of Robert Gaskins*, May 2012. [http://www.robertgaskins.com/], accessed December 19, 2012.

# Understanding the Book

The naming conventions in the book are simple. Acronyms, abbreviations and definitions are address in the table below.

One of the key features change in PowerPoint 2010 was the Microsoft Office® button in previous releases has been replace with the **File** tab.

The book module process steps, exercises, and review questions were developed on the Windows 7® platform.

## Acronyms, Abbreviations and Definitions

| Name/Symbol | Description |
| --- | --- |
| UI | User Interface - also known as the Ribbon |
| MOS | Microsoft Office Specialist |
| ☑ | Checked Mark – Enabled |
| ☐ | Unchecked Mark – Disabled |
| ◉ | Selected Radio Button – Enabled |
| ○ | Unselected Radio Button - Disabled |
| ▼ | Down Arrow – Displays drop down list |
| ⓘ | Information Icon |
| ❓ | Help Icon |

Table 1

## Basic Keyboard Shortcuts

| Name | Description of Keyboard Shortcuts |
| --- | --- |
| Undo | <Ctrl>+ <Z> |
| Cut | <Ctrl>+ <X> |
| Copy | <Ctrl>+ <C> |
| Paste | <Ctrl>+ <V> |
| Save | <Ctrl>+ <S> |
| Save, Close and Send | <Alt> + <S> |
| Print and Preview | <Ctrl>+ <P> |
| Search Inbox | <Ctrl>+ <E> |
| New Item | <Ctrl>+ <N> |
| Start Presentation at beginning | <F5> |
| Go to Next Slide | <SPACEBAR> |
| Stop or restart an automatic presentation. | <Ctrl>+ <L> |
| Go to Next Slide | SPACEBAR |
| Stop or restart an automatic presentation. | <Ctrl>+ <L> |
| Forward | <Ctrl>+ <F> |
| Help | <F1> |

Table 2

> **TIP:** There are additional keyboard shortcuts for PowerPoint 2010. Please refer to the following website for more information: http://office.microsoft.com/en-us/support/keyboard-shortcuts-for-use-while-creating-a-presentation-in-powerpoint-2010-HP010336519.aspx

## Easy Steps to PowerPoint 2010

# Understanding the Ribbon

The Ribbon User Interface (UI) is the key component to navigating and learning the PowerPoint 2010 application. It features tabular groups, commands and functional options. Its ease and use of similar style user interface will make it easier to learn and transition between the other Microsoft office products.

**Ribbon User Interface**

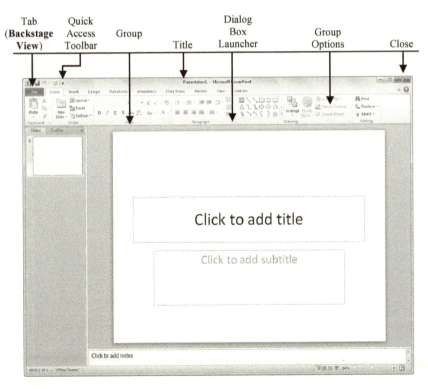

Figure 1

Module

1

# Easy Steps Understanding PowerPoint Environment

## OBJECTIVES

- Manage Presentation Views
- Manage Master Views
- Manage Presentation Windows
- Manage PowerPoint File options
- Backstage View
- Customize the Ribbon
- Manage the Quick Access Toolbar

## Understanding the PowerPoint Environment

This module will teach you the basics of managing the PowerPoint program environment and the presentation features of PowerPoint. You will learn how to configure various program options, navigate backstage view, adjust views, manage the presentation windows, configure quick access toolbar and configure PowerPoint slide options.

## Manage Views

These options will allow you to view presentation slides in different ways.

## Normal View:

**Step 1**: Select **View** tab and click on the **Normal** icon.

Figure 2

**Step 2**: The **PowerPoint** normal view pane will appear. The current slide will be in the right pane and the slides and outline schemas will be in the left pane.

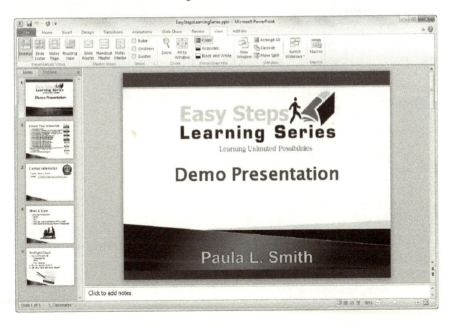

Figure 3

# Slide Sorter View:

**Step 1**: Select **View** tab and click on the **Slide Sorter** icon.

Figure 4

**Step 2**: The PowerPoint **Slide Sorter** view pane will appear.

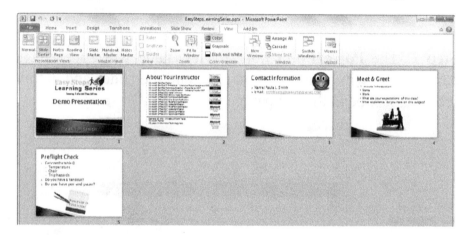

Figure 5

# Notes Page View:

**Step 1**: Select **View** tab and click on the **Notes Page** icon.

Figure 6

**Step 2**: The PowerPoint **Notes Page** view pane will appear.

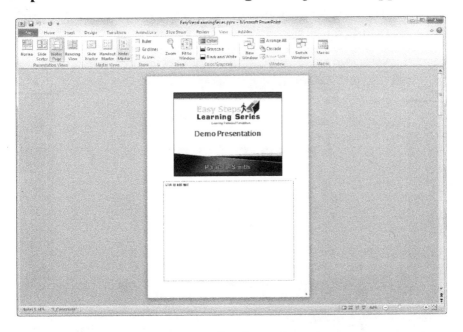

Figure 7

## Slide Show View:

**Step 1**: Select **View** tab and click on the **Reading View** icon or **F5** from the keyboard.

Figure 8

**Step 2**: The PowerPoint **Reading View** will appear. The slide show will start in the current window view.

Figure 9

# Manage Master Views

These options will allow you to view and edit slide, handout, and notes masters.

## Slide Master:

**Step 1**: Select **View** tab and click on the **Slide Master** icon.

Figure 10

# Manage Presentation Windows

## New Window:

**Step 1**: Select **View** tab and click on the **New Window** icon. A new window would be created. Select the **Arrange All** or **Cascade** icon to view.

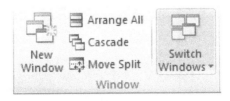

Figure 11

## Arrange All Windows:

**Step 1**: Select **View** tab and click on the **Arrange All** icon. All windows created will show in the view.

Figure 12

## Cascade Windows:

**Step 1**: Select **View** tab and click on the **Cascade** icon. All windows created will show in a stacked position for the view.

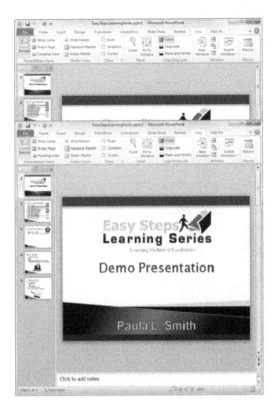

Figure 12

## Split Windows:

**Step 1**: Select **View** tab and click on the **Move Split** icon. This option will allow you to remove the splitters between windows. After Selection, the arrow will change to , drag to section to remove the split and enter to return to document.

## Manage PowerPoint File Options

These options will allow you to change general, proofing, save, language and advance settings in PowerPoint.

**Step 1**: Select **File** tab and click **Options** from the drop down list.

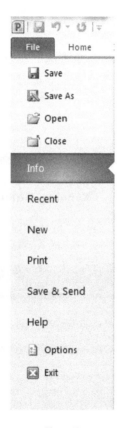

Figure 13

**Step 2**: The **PowerPoint** options dialog box will appear.

**Step 3:** Click on one of the options in the left pane to make changes to various **PowerPoint** environment settings and Click **OK** button to apply changes.

## General Settings:

This option will allow you to change general settings within PowerPoint.

## User Interface, Personalize your Microsoft Office, and Start up:

**Step 1**: Click on the check box ☑ to enable/disable Mini Toolbar or Live Preview.

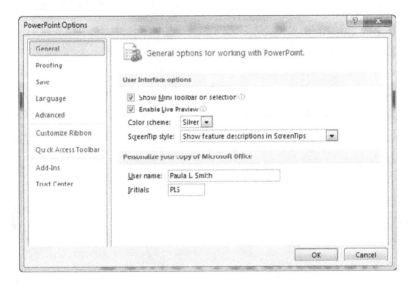

Figure 14

**Step 2**: Select the down arrow ▼ to change options from drop down list for color scheme and screen tip styles.

**Step 3**: Enter your User name and Initials to personalize your Microsoft Office in the input dialog box. Click the **OK** button to apply changes.

## Proofing Settings:

This option will allow you to change how PowerPoint corrects and formats your text.

**Step 1**: Click **AutoCorrect Options** button to correct and format text as you type.

**Step 2**: Click on the check box ☑ to enable/disable when correcting spelling options in Microsoft Office programs. Select the **Custom Dictionaries** button to customized dictionaries and select the down arrow ▼ to pick from the drop down list for **French** and **Spanish modes**.

**Step 3**: Click on the check box ☑ to enable/disable when correcting spelling options in PowerPoint. Click the **OK** button to apply changes.

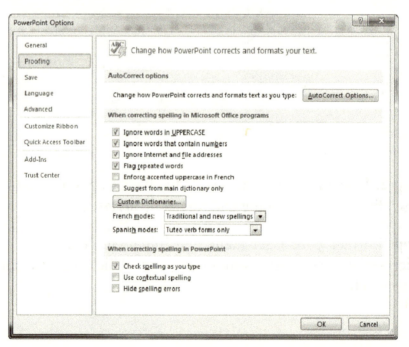

Figure 15

## Save Settings:

This option will allow you to customize how presentations are saved.

**Step 1:** Select the down arrow 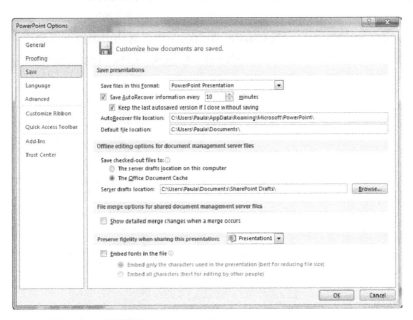 to pick from the drop down list to save files in a specified **PowerPoint Presentation** format.

**Step 2:** Click on the check box ☑ to enable/disable save auto recover information and keep the last auto saved version if close without saving options.

**Step 3:** Enter in the save auto recover information specified minutes in dialog box when option is enabled. Enter directory locations for auto recover and default files.

Figure 16

**Step 4:** Click on the check box 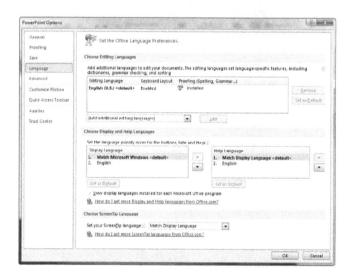 to enable/disable checked-out files to option. Whenever drafts location is enabled, select the **Browse** button for directory location.

**Step 5:** Click on the check box ☑ to enable/disable file merged options and embed fonts in the file. Click the **OK** button to apply changes.

## Language Settings:

This option will allow you to set the language preferences for editing, display, and help languages.

**Step 1:** Select the down arrow [Add additional editing languages] ▼ to enter additional languages from the drop down list.

**Step 2:** Select the **Remove** to remove a language or **Set as Default** button when enabled. Click **OK** button to apply changes.

Figure 17

## Advanced Settings

This option will allow you to change additional options in working with PowerPoint environment. We will not cover this section because some of the options have been covered in previous sections of this module.

## Customize the Ribbon

This option will allow you to add and remove popular commands on specified Tabs and Groups.

**Step 1:** Click on the **New Tab** or **New Group** button to add a tab or group.

**Step 2:** Click on the **Rename** button to change a name of a tab or group. Click the **OK** button to apply changes.

**Step 3:** Change the order of the **Tab** or **Group** by selecting the up or down arrows to the right of the right panel.

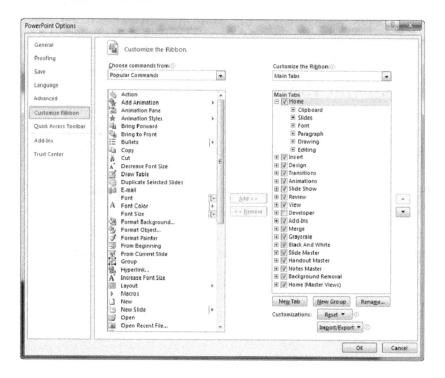

Figure 18

**Step 4:** Customization of the Ribbon is click away. Click on the **Import/Export** button to import files or export your customize ribbon to other programs on your computer. Click on the **Reset** button to reset all customizations.

# Configure the Quick Access Toolbar

This option will allow you to add and remove popular commands on the **Quick Access Toolbar**.

**Step 1:** Click on the **Add** or **Remove** button to add or remove a command to the **Quick Access Toolbar.**

**Step 2:** Change the order of the commands on the **Quick Access Toolbar** by selecting the up or down arrows to the right of the right panel.

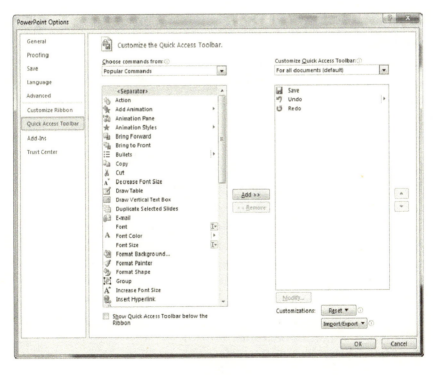

Figure 19

**Step 3:** Customization of the **Quick Access Toolbar** is a click away. Click on the **Import/Export** button to import files or export your customize ribbon to other programs on your computer. Click on the **Reset** button to reset all customizations.

## Trust Center Settings

This option will allow you change some of the security settings but it is not recommended you change any of the defaulted ones. This section will only focus on Active-x, Macro, and Protected View settings.

**Step 1:** Select **File** tab and click on **Options** from the drop down list.

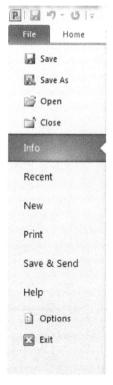

Figure 20

**Step 2**: The **PowerPoint** options dialog box will appear.

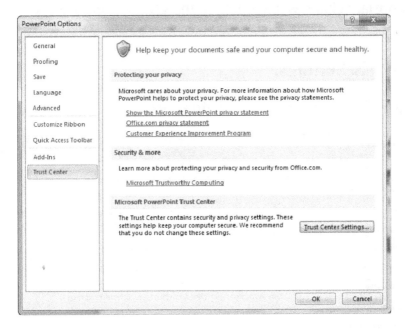

Figure 21

**Step 3:** Click on **Trust Center** option in the left pane. Select the **Trust Center Settings** button.

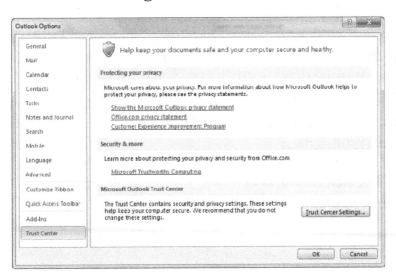

Figure 22

**Step 4:** The **Trust Center** dialog box will appear. Make the appropriate changes and click on the **OK** button to apply changes.

## Active-X Settings:

**Step 1:** Select the **ActiveX Settings** option from the left pane.

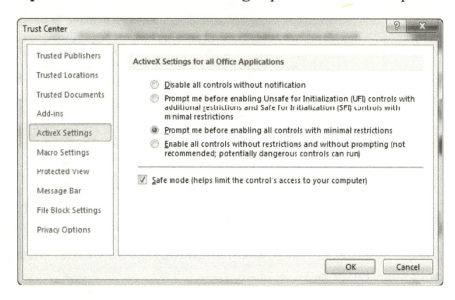

Figure 23

**Step 2:** Click on the radio button◉ to disable all controls without notification, enable prompts before enabling Unsafe for Initialization controls, enable all controls with minimal restrictions, and enable all controls without restrictions and without prompting.

**Step 3:** Click on the check box ☑ to enable/disable safe mode option. Click the **OK** button to apply changes.

## Macro Settings:

**Step 1:** Select the **Macro Settings** option from the left pane.

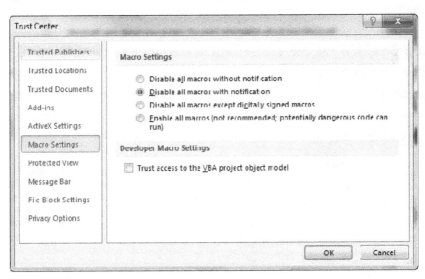

Figure 24

**Step 2:** Click on the radio button⊙ to disable all macros without notification, with notification, except digitally signed macros, or enable all macros.

**Step 3:** Click on the check box ☑ to enable/disable trust access to the VBA project object model. Click the **OK** button to apply changes.

## Protected View Settings:

**Step 1:** Select the **Protected View Settings** option from the left pane.

**Step 2:** Click on the check box ☑ to enable/disable protected view for files originating from the Internet, files located in potentially unsafe locations and Outlook attachments options and data execution prevention mode.  Click the **OK** button to apply changes.

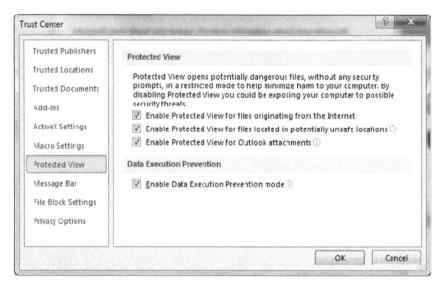

Figure 25

# Backstage View

The backstage view of PowerPoint is where you manage permissions, prepare for sharing, and manage PowerPoint versions.

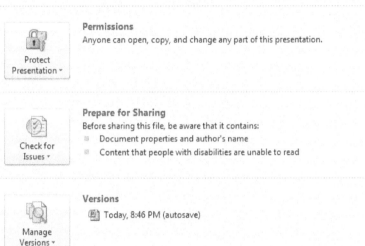

Figure 26

## Protect Presentation

This option will allow you to mark presentations as final, encrypt with password, restrict permission by people, and add a digital signature.

**Step 1**: Click on the **Protect Presentation** icon.

**Step 2**: Drop down list will appear and choose one of the options.

Figure 27

## Mark a presentation as Final:

**Step 1**: After clicking on the **Protect Presentation** icon, select **Mark as Final** option from drop down list.

**Step 2**: The general dialog box will appear asking *"This presentation will be marked as final and then saved."* Click the **OK** button to mark as final.

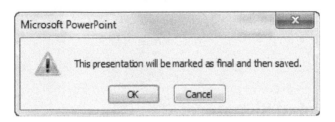

Figure 28

## Encrypt with Password:

**Step 1**: After clicking on the **Protect Presentation** icon, select **Encrypt with Password** option from drop down list.

**Step 2**: The **Encrypt Document** dialog box will appear. Enter password in the input box. Click the **OK** button to apply changes.

Figure 29

# Restrict Permission by People:

**Step 1**: After clicking on the **Protect Presentation** icon, select **Restrict Permission by People** option from drop down list.

**Step 2**: Click on **Unrestricted Access, Restricted Access,** or **Manage Credentials** options to restrict permission.

Figure 30

# Add a Digital Signature:

**Step 1**: After clicking on the **Protect Presentation** icon, select **Add a Digital Signature** option from drop down list.

**Step 2**: The **Microsoft PowerPoint** dialog box will appear. Click **OK** button to continue or **Signature Services from the Office Marketplace** button.

Figure 31

**Step 3**: After you select the **OK** button, click on the radio button◉ to select either option. Click **OK** button to continue with selected option.

Figure 32

# Prepare for Sharing

This will allow for you to check for issues when sharing PowerPoint presentation for compatibility and accessibility.

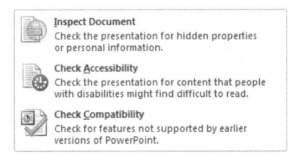

Figure 33

## Inspect Document:

**Step 1**: Select **Inspect Document** option from drop down list.

**Step 2**: The **Document Inspector** dialog box will appear.

Figure 34

**Step 3**: Click the **Inspect** button and review the inspection results will appear. Click the **Close** button to exit or apply changes from inspection.

Figure 35

# Manage Versions

This option will allow for you to recover unsaved or delete all unsaved presentations.

**Step 1**: Select **Recover Unsaved Presentations** option from drop down list.

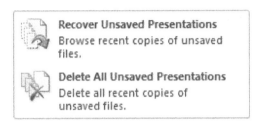

Figure 36

**Step 2**: Browse from the directory folder to recover and select file.

**Step 3**: Select **Delete All Unsaved Presentations** option from drop down list. The *"Are you sure you want to delete all copies of unsaved files?"* message will appear. Click on **Yes** to proceed with delete process or **No** to cancel.

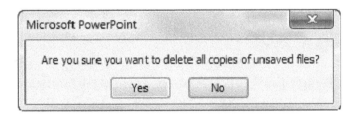

Figure 37

# Module 1:
# Practice Steps

## Interactive Practice Exercises:

**Step 1:** Create a blank presentation.  Select the **Metro** theme. Save as a template and name it "**My New Template**".

**Step 2**: Create a new presentation from the Business template. Save the new presentation with the name "**My Business Presentation**".

**Step 3:** Create a new blank presentation.  Create a master slide layout.  Select the newly created master slide in new presentation. Save new presentation with the name" **My New Master**".

**Step 4:** Open the **My New Master** presentation and duplicate the third slide and change the title to **"I have just duplicated this slide"**.

**Step 5:** View the "**My Business Presentation**" with the Slide Sorter option.

**Step 6:** Change the **User Interface** color scheme to blue in the **Backstage** view.

**Step 7:** Change the **Quick Access Toolbar** to include the following commands: **New, Save, Save As, Undo** and **Print**.

**Step 8:** Change the **User Interface** color scheme to blue in the **Backstage** view.

Module

2

# Easy Steps in Understanding Slide Presentations

## OBJECTIVES

- Create a Presentation
- Create and Edit Photo Albums
- Apply Slide Size and orientation settings
- Arrange Slides
- Format Slides
- Enter and Format Text
- Format Text Boxes

## Understanding Slide Presentations

This module will teach you the basics of slide presentations. Some of the features you will learn are how to create and edit photo albums, create and edit photo albums, apply slide size and orientation settings, add and remove slides, format slides, enter and format text, and format text boxes.

## What is a Presentation?

A PowerPoint presentation is a way of displaying ideas, concepts and illustrations using graphics, pictures, text and any other contextual object on slides. The slides are arranged in a logical sense to demonstrate the idea, concept, thoughts and illustrations. This is called a slide show presentation.

Compare the analogy of a new home for sale similar to a presentation. It is a physical structure that can be accessed, managed or updated. It houses information of people who reside in it. You can access the home through the front, back or side door, manage it by cleaning, organizing and have the control of who can come in or stay out. You may even update the exterior with new paint, landscape or add on a room to give it a new look.

Figure 38

## Create a Presentation

This option will allow you to create a presentation from a blank template or an existing template.

## Create a Presentation from a Blank Template:

**Step 1:** Select the **New** option on the **File** Tab.

Figure 39

**Step 2:** The **Available Templates** and **Themes** dialog box will appear.

## Step 3: Select the **Blank presentation** icon.

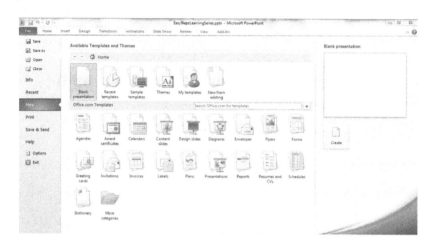

Figure 40

## Step 4: Click on the **Create** button. A new presentation window will appear. You are ready to begin.

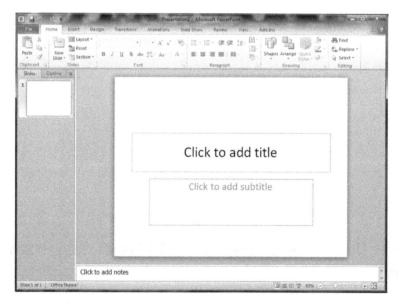

Figure 41

# Create a Presentation from a Ready Made Design Template:

**Step 1:** Select the **New** option on the **File** Tab.

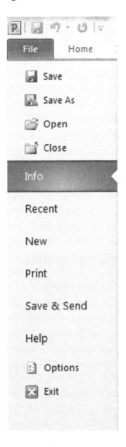

Figure 42

**Step 2:** The **Available Templates** and **Themes** dialog box will appear.

**Step 3:** Select from **sample templates, themes, previous save templates** or one of the **online office.com templates**. (*For Example:* Select an Award Certificates category)

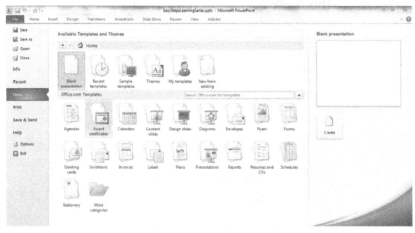

Figure 43

**Step 4:** The **Award Certificates templates** dialog box will appear. Select a template from the **Business award** folder.

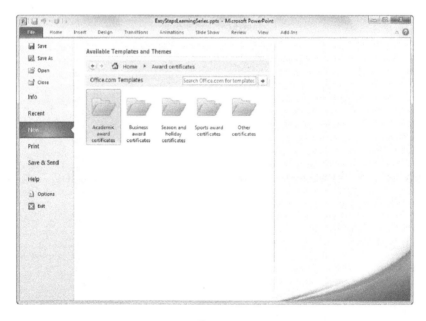

Figure 44

**Step 5:** Select on the **Employee performance award** template icon. Click on the **Download** button.

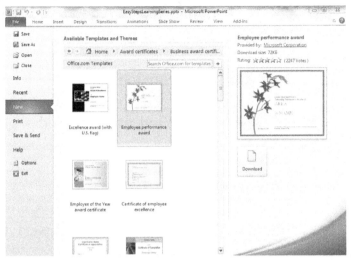

Figure 45

**Step 6:** The **Employee performance award** dialog box will appear. Make changes or save the presentation

**Step 7:** Select the **File** tab and click on **Save** or **Save As** option to save the new **Employee performance award** presentation.

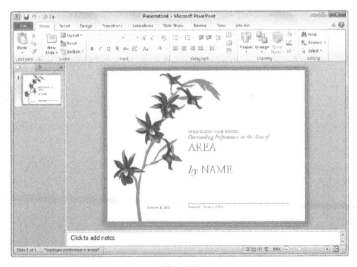

Figure 46

## Create a Presentation from an Outline

This option will allow you to create a presentation from an outline can be either a *Word* document (.doc or .docx) or a *Rich Text Format* file (.rtf)

**Step 1**: Open a **New Blank** presentation.

**Step 2**: Click the **New Slide** option from the **Slides** group on the **Home** tab.

**Step 3**: Select **Slides from Outline** option.

**Step 4**: Select the **File** to convert from the **Insert Outline** dialog box.

**Step 5**: Click the **Insert button.**

**Step 6**: The Outline will be converted in the open presentation.

# Create and Edit Photo Albums

This option will allow you to create and edit presentations based upon a set of pictures.

## Create a Photo Album:

**Step 1:** Click on the **Photo Album** option from the **Illustrations** group on the **Insert** tab.

Figure 47

**Step 2:** Select **New Photo Album** from the drop down list.

Figure 48

**Step 3:** Click on the **File/Disk button.**

Figure 49

**Step 4:** Browse to directory of pictures, select picture, and click the Insert button.

Figure 50

**Step 5:** Add as many pictures you want in the new photo album.

Figure 51

**Step 5:** Select the **Create** button to finish and create the new photo album with selected preferences.

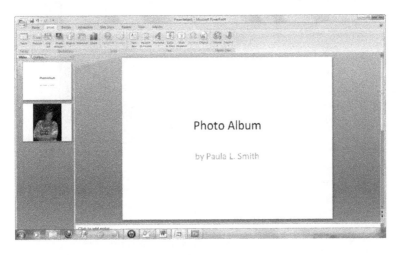

Figure 52

# Edit a Photo Album:

**Step 1:** Open the photo album you want to edit.

**Step 2:** Click on the **Photo Album** option from the **Illustrations** group on the **Insert** tab.

Figure 53

**Step 3:** Select **Edit Photo Album** from the drop down list.

Figure 54

**Step 4:** The **Edit Photo Album** dialog box will appear. Click on the **Update** button to apply changes.

Figure 55

## Apply Slide Size and Orientation Settings

This option will allow you to change slide size and slides, notes, handouts, and outline orientation.

## Page Setup to change Slide Size:

**Step 1:** Click on **Page Setup** icon from the **Page Setup** group on the **Design** tab.

Figure 56

**Step 2:** The **Page Setup** dialog box will appear.

**Step 3:** Select the down arrow and choose from drop down list or enter manually the width and height. Click the **OK** button to apply changes.

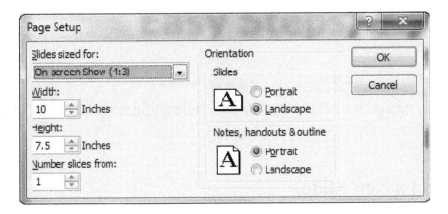

Figure 57

# Slide Orientation

This option will help you select n orientation of a presentation.

**Step 1:** Click on **Slide Orientation** icon from the **Page Setup** group on the **Design** tab.

Figure 58

**Step 2:** Select from the drop down list **portrait** or **landscape** orientation.

Figure 59

## Arrange Slides

This option will allow you to add, delete and arrange slides in a presentation.

## Add a New Slide:

**Step 1**: Click on the **New Slide** icon from the **Slides** group on the **Home** tab.

**Step 2**: Select the type of **New Slide** from the drop down list. The options are title slide, title and content, duplicate selected slide, slide from outline or reuse a slide from another presentation.

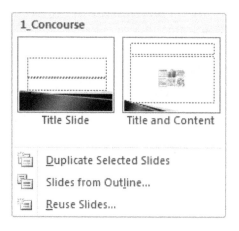

Figure 60

# Delete a Slide:

**Step 1**: Click on the **Slide** you want to delete.

**Step 2**: Click the **Cut** ✂ icon or Right-click and select **Delete Slide** option.

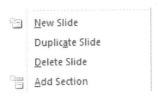

Figure 61

# Duplicate a slide:

**Step 1:** Click on the **New Slide** icon from the **Slides** group on the **Home** tab.

**Step 2**: Click on **Duplicate Selected Slides** and the new slide is added to your presentation.

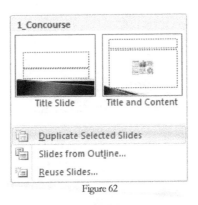

Figure 62

**TIP:** Select the slide to duplicate right-click and select the duplicate slide option.

## Rearrange slides:

**Step 1:** Select **Slide** on the **Slides** tab in the left pane. Drag and drop before or after the slide number you desired.

**Step 2:** Select **Slide number** on the **Outline** tab in the left pane. Drag and drop before or after the slide number you desired.

## Format Slides

This option will show you how to format section, modify themes, select slide layout, apply fill color, gradient, picture, texture or pattern to a slide and set up header and footers.

## Slide Layout:

**Step 1:** Click on the **Layout** icon from the **Slides** group on the **Home** tab.

Figure 63

**Step 2:** Click on the layout you want and it will modify the existing slide you selected for the change.

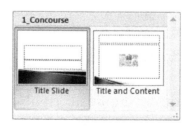

Figure 64

## Design Themes:

**Step 1:** Select the **Design** tab.

**Step 2:** Click on a **Theme** from the **Themes** group to apply to your presentation.

Figure 65

**Step 3:** You can change the **Color**, **Fonts** and **Effects** of a theme. Select the down arrow ⏷ on any of these options to change. You may select one of the built-in color schemes or create a new one.

**Step 4:** Select the down arrow ⏷ for more **Themes** selections from the **Themes** group, from Microsoft Office® Online or your local computer.

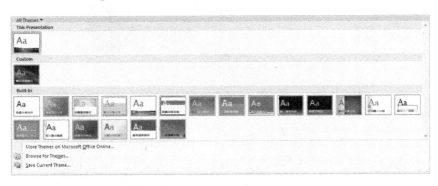

Figure 66

## Format Background:

**Step 1:** Select **Background Styles** option from the **Background** group on the **Design** tab.

Figure 67

**Step 2:** Select **Format Background** option from the drop down list.

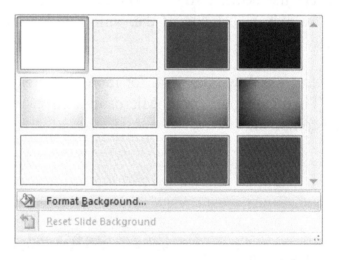

Figure 68

**Step 3:** The **Format Background** dialog box will appear. You may select a **Fill** or **Picture** type for your background.

**Step 4:** The **Format Background** dialog box will appear. You may select a **Fill** or **Picture** type for your background.

Figure 69

**Step 5:** The **Format Background** dialog box will appear. You may select a **Fill** or **Picture** type for your background.

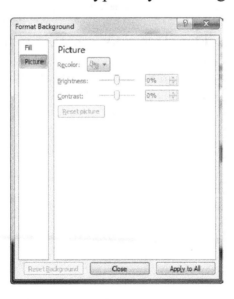

Figure 70

## Setting up Header and Footer:

**Step 1**: Click on the e-mail message you want to add a reminder. Select the **Follow Up** option from the **Tags** group on the **Home** tab.

**Step 2:** Select **Add Reminder** option from the drop down list.

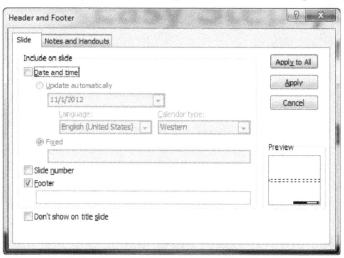

Figure 71

---

**TIP:** Select **Clear Flag** option to remove the flagged reminder from e-mail message.

---

## Enter and Format Text

This option will allow you to enter and format text on slide.

## Insert a Text Box on a Slide:

**Step 1**: Click on the text box on the slide and begin typing if you are using a slide master format.

**TIP:** A new slide created from a slide master will have the text boxes already on the slide. Click anywhere within the text box and begin entering text.

Figure 72

**Step 2**: Click on the **Text box**.

**Step 3:** Drag the **Text box** on the slide. Enter your text.

**Modifying text on a slide:**

**Step 1**: Select the text you want to change or drag your mouse over text to highlight.

Figure 73

**Step 2**: Select from following options to change text:
- Select text by **Double-Clicking** it.
- Press the **Delete** key to remove selected text.
- Press the **Backspace** key to remove selected text.
- Undo a change to selected text; click the **Undo** button on the Quick Access Toolbar.
- Use the **Cut, Copy** or **Paste** buttons to modify or delete text.

**Step 3**: **Right-Click** on the selected or highlighted text.

**Step 4**: A **Drop-down** list of options will appear. Select from options to make change to selected or highlighted text.

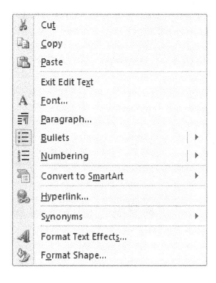

Figure 74

# Formatting text on a slide:

**Step 1**: Select the text you want to **Format**.

**Step 2**: Select the **Format** tab. **Click** on a **Text Fill and Text Outline** or **Text Effects** option.

Figure 75

## Format text with Text Fill:

**Step 1**: Select the text you want to **Format**.

**Step 2**: Click on a **Text Fill** down arrow .

**Step 3**: A list of **Text Fill** options will appear in a dialog box.

Figure 76

**Step 4**: Select one of the **Text Fill** options to apply to selected text. The change will appear instantly.

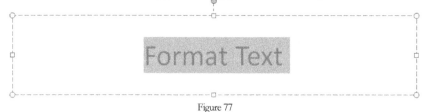

Figure 77

## Format text with Text Outline:

**Step 1**: Select the text you want to **Format**.

**Step 2**: Click on a **Text Outline** down arrow 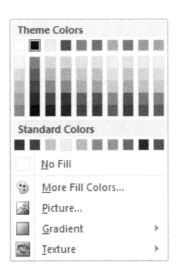 Text Outline ▾ .

**Step 3**: A list of **Text Outline** options will appear in a dialog box.

Figure 78

**Step 4:** Select one of the **Text Outline** options to apply to selected text. The change will appear instantly.

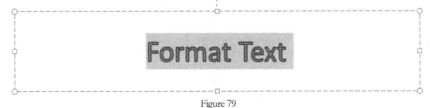

Figure 79

## Format text with Text Effects:

**Step 1**: Select the text you want to **Format**.

**Step 2**: Click on the **Text Effects** down arrow 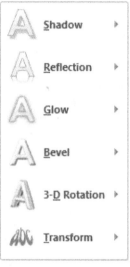.

**Step 3**: A list of **Text Effects** options will appear in a dialog box.

Figure 80

**Step 4:** Select one of the **Text Effects** options to apply to selected text. The change will appear instantly.

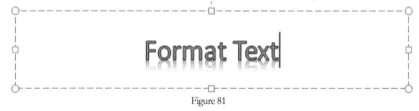

Figure 81

## Format Text Boxes:

**Step 1**: Select the **Text Box** you want to format.

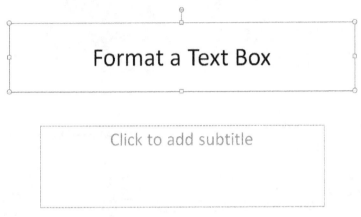

Figure 82

**Step 2**: Select a **Shape style** option to change the border of the text box.

Figure 83

**Step 3**: After selection, the text box color change will display instantly.

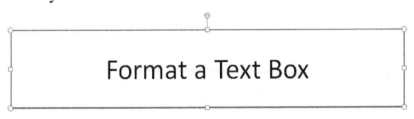

Figure 84

**Step 4**: Select the **Shape Fill** option to change inside color of the text box.

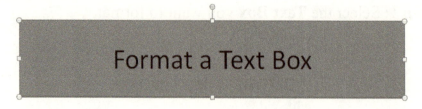

Figure 85

**Step 5**: Select **Picture**, **Gradient** or **Textures** options to change inside appearance of the box.

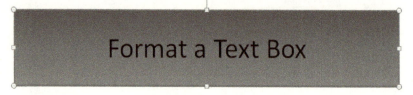

Figure 86

# Module 2:
# Practice Steps

## Interactive Practice Exercises

**Step 1:** Create a blank presentation. Click the slide's **Click to add title** placeholder in the slide pane. Enter the title "**My Presentation**", format size 24 and change the color to red. Add a subtitle called "**How to Insert a New Text Box.**" Select the **Metro** theme. Save it as a template and name it "**My New Template**".

**Step 2**: Create a new presentation from the Business template. Save the new presentation with the name "**My Business Presentation**".

**Step 3**: Create a new presentation from a "**Family Reunion**" template. Add your family information. Click the **Save As** button and name the file "**Your Name Family Reunion**".

**Step 4**: Create a new photo album. Add pictures and save as "**My New Photo Album**".

**Step 5:** Open a **Business Card** template and add your information and format text to color dark blue. Add hyperlink to your email address.

**Step 6:** Create a new presentation. Add the title "**Learning PowerPoint**". Change font size to 36, font to Cooper Black, color to dark blue and shape effect of outer offset bottom shadow.

**Step 7:** Create a New Blank presentation with the "**Lists to Do Checklist**" template and populate it with your information.

Module

3

# Easy Steps in Understanding Graphical and Multimedia Elements

## OBJECTIVES

- Manage Graphical Elements
- Manage Images
- Manage WordArt and Shapes
- Manage SmartArt
- Manage Video and Audio content

# Understanding Managing Graphical and Multimedia Elements

This module will teach you the basics of managing graphical and multimedia elements on a slide. Some of the elements will include drawing elements, shapes and quick styles of drawing elements, movies and sounds.

## Manage Graphical Elements

This option allows you to add, arrange, and format graphical drawing elements on a slide.

## Add drawing elements to a slide:

**Step 1**: Select the **Home** tab and select drawing element you want to add to slide from the **Drawing** group.

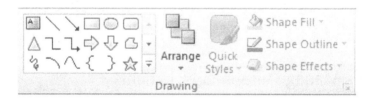

Figure 87

**Step 2**: Click **up or down arrow button** to view selection of drawing elements.

**Step 3:** Select element and drag it to the slide and then click to release it.

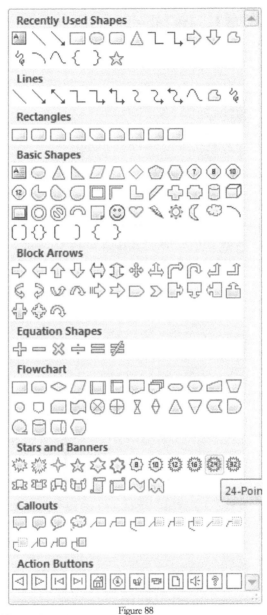

Figure 88

## Arrange drawing elements on a slide:

**Step 1**: Select the **Home** tab and click on the **Arrange** icon from the **Drawing** group.

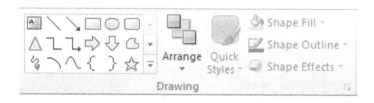

Figure 89

**Step 2**: The drop down list will display to order, group or position objects on the slide. Select one of the arrange option from the drop down list.

Figure 90

## Add Quick Styles to graphical elements on a slide:

**Step 1**: Select the **Home** tab and select **Quick Styles** icon from the **Drawing** group.

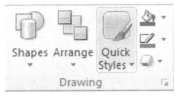

Figure 91

**TIP:** You can change any drawing element appearance by **Shape Fill, Shape Outline** and **Shape Effects**.

**Step 2**: The drop down list will display various styles. Select fill option from the drop down list.

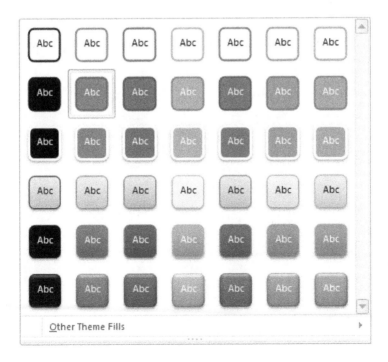

Figure 92

**Step 3**: After selection, the drawing element change will display instantly.

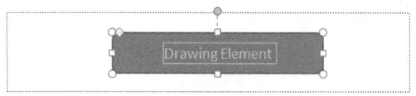

Figure 93

# Manage Images

This option allows you to place images or pictures on slides. Apply color adjustments, image corrections, adding effects to images, cropping, compressing, and resetting pictures.

## Add a picture to a slide:

**Step 1**: Select **Insert** tab and click on the **Picture** icon from the **Images** group.

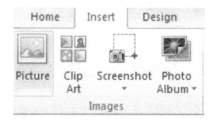

Figure 94

**Step 2:** The **Insert Picture** dialog box will appear.

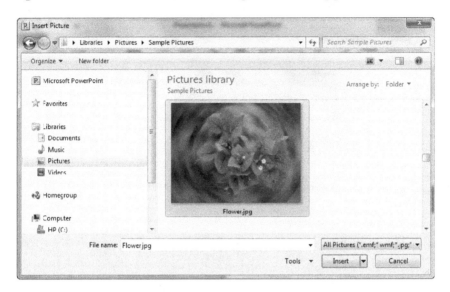

Figure 95

**Step 3:** Select the image or picture and click on the **Insert** button to apply change. The picture will display on the slide.

# Add a Clip Art to a slide:

**Step 1:** Select **Insert** tab and click on the **Clip Art** icon from the **Images** group.

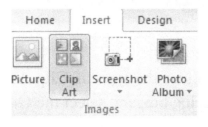

Figure 96

**Step 2:** The **Clip Art** task pane will appear on the right.

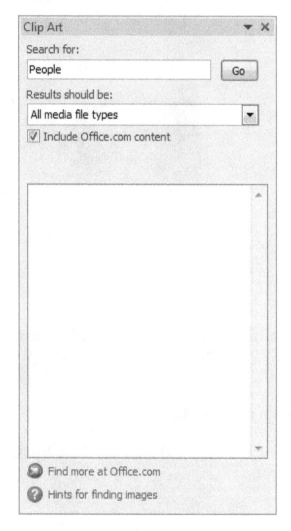

Figure 97

**Step 3:** You can enter the type of **Clip Art** to search for in the **Search for** dialog box and select the **Go** button ._Go_ .

**Step 4:** You can select the type of results in the **Results should be** dialog box, by selecting the down arrow ▾.

**Step 5:** Select the image or picture and click on the **Insert** button to apply change. The picture will display on the slide.

Figure 98

## Manage WordArt and Shapes

This option allows you manage **WordArt** and **Shape**s on a slide. Apply **WordArt** style to selected text or all text in the shape.

## Add WordArt Style to a slide:

**Step 1**: Select the text you want to **Format**.

**Step 2**: Click on the **WordArt Styles icon** down arrow ⏷.

**Step 3**: A list of **WordArt Styles** options will appear in a dialog box.

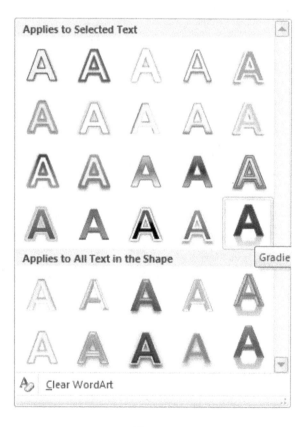

Figure 99

**Step 4:** Select one of the **WordArt Styles** to apply to selected text or all text in the shape. The change will appear instantly.

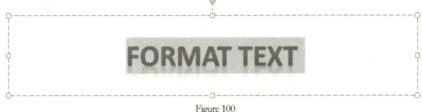

Figure 100

### Clear WordArt Style from text on a slide:

**Step 1**: Select the text with the formatted **WordArt.**
**Step 2**: Click on a **WordArt Styles** down arrow ⏷.

**Step 3**: Select the **Clear WordArt**  A↙ Clear WordArt
option to reset format options.

## Manage SmartArt

This option allows you to manage **SmartArt** elements on a slide to communicate information in a visual way.

## Insert SmartArt diagram to a slide:

**Step 1:** Select **Insert** tab and click on the **SmartArt** icon from the **Illustrations** group.

Figure 101

**Step 2:** The **Choose** a **SmartArt Graphic** dialog box will appear.

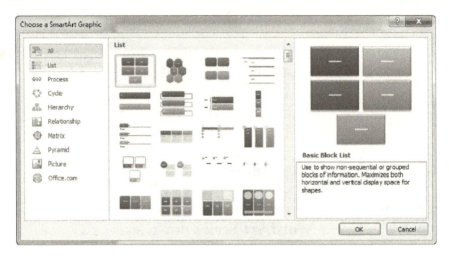

Figure 102

**Step 3**: Select the **SmartArt** graphic you want and click the **OK** button to apply graphic to the slide. You can add text, change colors, format the shape, etc.

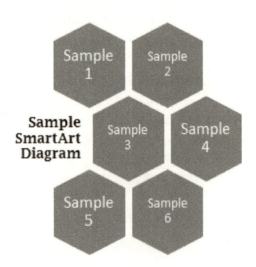

Figure 103

# Modify a SmartArt Graphic:

**Step 1**: Select **SmartArt** element on your slide.

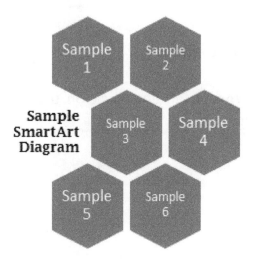

Figure 104

**Step 2**: The **SmartArt** tool will appear. Select the **Design** or the **Format** tab to make appropriate changes.

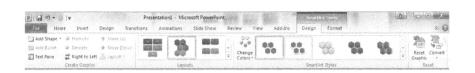

Figure 105

## Manage Video and Audio Content

This option allows you to create and manage video and audio content on a slide.

### Add a Video to a slide:

**Step 1**: Select **Insert** tab and click on the **Video** icon from the **Media** group.

Figure 106

**Step 2**: Select options from a **Video from File, Video from Web Site** or **Clip Art Video**.

Figure 107

### Add a **Video from File** to a slide:

**Step 1**: Select **Insert** tab and click on the **Video** icon from the **Media** group.

**Step 2**: Select the option **Video from File**.

**Step 3**: The **Insert Video** dialog box will appear.

Figure 108

**Step 4**: Select the image or picture and click on the **Insert** button to apply the change.

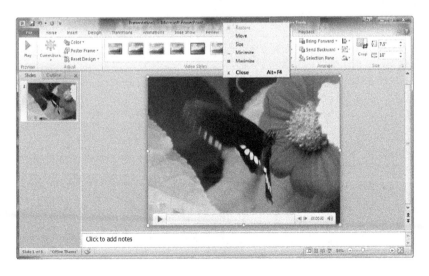

Figure 109

## Add a Video from Web Site to a slide:

**Step 1**: Select **Insert** tab and click on the **Video** icon from the **Media** group.

**Step 2**: Select the option **Video from Web Site**.

Figure 110

**Step 3**: The **Insert Video from Web Site** dialog box will appear.

Figure 111

**Step 4**: Insert the link to the video in the dialog box or copy the embedded code from web site. Click on the **Insert** button to apply to change.

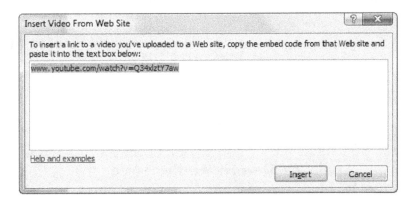

Figure 112

# Add Clip Art Video to a slide:

**Step 1**: Select **Insert** tab and click on the **Video** icon from the **Media** group.

**Step 2**: Select the option **Clip Art Video**.

Figure 113

## Add Audio to a slide:

**Step 1**: Select **Insert** tab and Click on the **Audio** option.

Figure 114

**Step 2**: You have the option to select an **Audio from File, Clip Art Audio** or **Record Audio**. Select the option and click the **OK** button to continue.

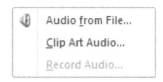

Figure 115

## Add Audio from File to a slide:

**Step 1**: Select **Insert** tab and Click on the **Audio** option.

Figure 116

**Step 2**: Select an **Audio from File** option.

**Step 3:** The **Insert Audio** dialog box will appear. Browse to the selected file and Click the **Insert** button to apply audio file to the slide.

Figure 117

# Add Clip Art Audio to a slide:

**Step 1**: Select **Insert** tab and Click on the **Audio** option.

Figure 118

**Step 2**: The **Clip Art Audio** dialog box will appear.

**Step 3:** Search for the **Clip Art Audio** file. Select the **Clip Art Audio** file by dragging it to the slide or right-click and select the **Insert** option.

Figure 119

# Module 3: Practice Steps

## Interactive Practice Exercises:

**Step 1:** Create a **New Blank** presentation. Add a **Movie** file from the Clip Art Organizer. Add a header with "**My New Movie Presentation** and footer with date and page number.

**Step 2:** Create a **New Blank** presentation. Insert a textual list. Convert it to a Smart Art graphic. Save as "**My New Smart Art**".

**Step 3:** Open the "**My New Smart Art**" presentation. Insert two new slides. Insert an organizational chart on one slide, a relationship smart art graphic on the other and save the presentation as "**My New Smart Art # 2**".

**Step 4:** Create a **New Blank** presentation. Insert a photo from the Clip Art organizer. Save as "**My New Photo**".

**Step 5:** Create a new presentation. Add the title "**Learning PowerPoint** and apply the word style "**Fill - Red, Accent 2, Matte Bevel**".

**Step 6:** Create a **New Blank** presentation. Insert a photo from the Clip Art organizer and save as "**My New Photo**".

**Step 7:** Open the "**My New Photo**" presentation. Insert two new slides. Insert a slide with a Photo Album. Insert a slide with a Clip Art and save as "**My New Photo# 2**".

Module

4

# Easy Steps in Understanding Charts and Tables

## OBJECTIVES

- Create and Manage Tables
- Create and Manage Charts
- Apply Chart Elements
- Manage Chart Layouts
- Manage Chart Elements

## Understanding Charts and Tables

This module will teach you the basics of charts and tables. It will help you learn to create, modify, and manage charts and tables in presentations.

## Create and Manage Tables

This option will allow you to insert, modify and manage tables on a slide.

## Insert a table on a slide:

**Step 1:** Select **Insert** tab and click on the **Tables** icon from the **Tables** group.

Figure 120

**Step 2:** The **Insert Table** dialog box will appear.

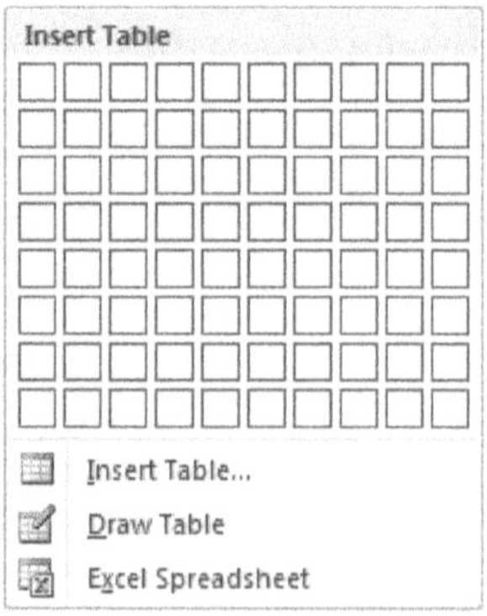

Figure 121

**Step 3**: Select the **Insert Table** option or **Drag** your mouse over the cells for number of rows and columns for table. Make sure the selection is highlighted.

**Step 4**: Select the **Insert Table** option.    The table will be inserted on the slide.

Figure 122

# Draw a table on a slide:

**Step 1:** Select **Insert** tab and click on the **Tables** icon from the **Tables** group.

Figure 123

**Step 2:** The **Insert Table** dialog box will appear.

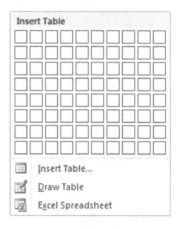

Figure 124

**Step 3:** Select the **Draw Table** option. The cursor will turn into pen mode and the **Table Tool** options will appear.

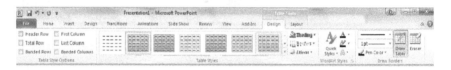

Figure 125

**Step 4:** Click on the slide and start drawing the table in pen mode.

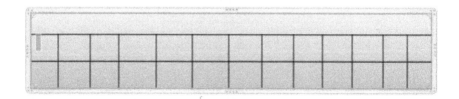

Figure 126

## Import an Excel spreadsheet and insert as a table on a slide:

**Step 1:** Select **Insert tab** and click on the **Tables** icon from the **Tables** group.

Figure 127

**Step 2:** The **Insert Table** dialog box will appear.

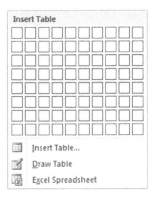

Figure 128

**Step 3:** Select the **Excel Spreadsheet** option. The cursor will turn into pen mode 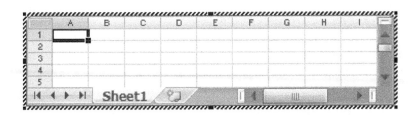. The **Table Tool** option appears.

Figure 129

**Step 4:** A blank **Excel** spreadsheet or workbook will be inserted on the slide.

## Modify a table on a slide:

**Step 1**: Select **Table** element on your slide and change options.

**Step 2**: You can right-click to also change options.

# Create and Manage Charts

This option will allow you to create and modify charts; apply chart elements, chart layouts, chart styles and format charts.

## Create a chart and insert on a slide:

**Step 1:** Select **Insert** tab and click on the **Chart** option.

Figure 130

**Step 2:** The **Insert Chart** dialog box will appear. Select a **Chart** from the options.

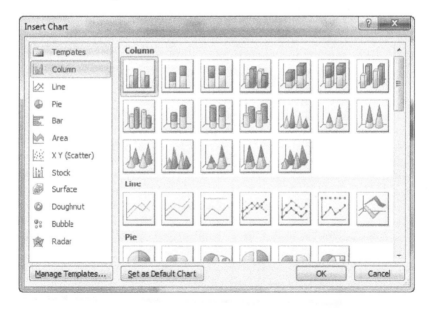

Figure 131

**Step 3:** Click the **OK** button to insert the **Chart** on a slide.

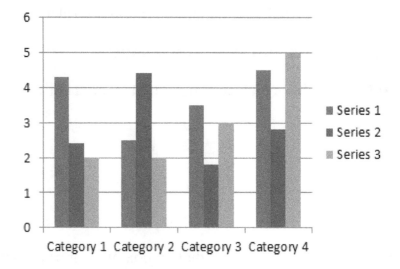

Figure 132

# Insert an existing chart on a slide:

**Step 1**: Select **Insert** tab and click on the **Chart** option. The **Insert Chart** dialog box will appear.

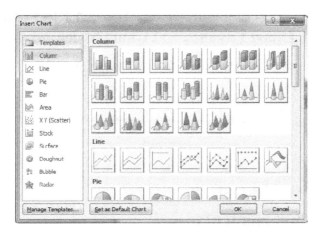

Figure 133

**Step 2:** Select the **Manage Templates** button. The browse folder directory dialog box will appear.

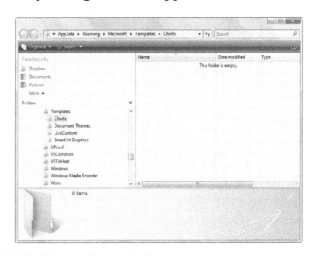

Figure 134

**Step 3:** Select the **Charts** file to add to the slide.

## Modify a chart to a slide:

**Step 1**: Select **Chart** element on your slide.

**Step 2**: The **Chart** tool will appear.  You can select options from **Type**, **Data**, **Chart Layouts,** and **Chart Styles** groups.

Figure 135

## Apply Chart elements

## Add a picture to a chart:

**Step 1**: Select the **Picture** icon from the **Insert** group on the **Layout** tab.

Figure 136

**Step 2**: The **Insert Picture dialog box** will appear. Select a picture from folder. Click the **Insert** button to apply changes.

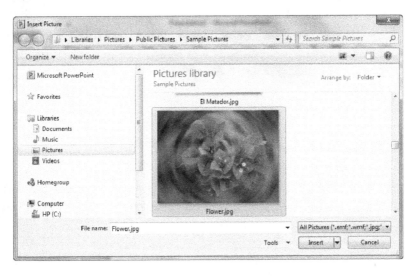

Figure 137

**Step 3**: The **Picture** will appear on chart. You can position the picture anywhere on the chart.

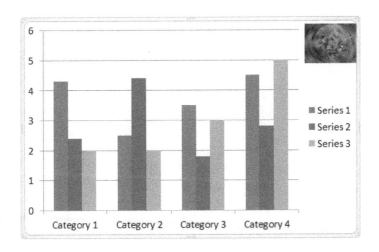

Figure 138

## Add a shape to a chart:

**Step 1**: Select the **Shape** icon from the **Insert** group on the **Layout** tab.

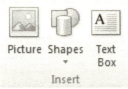

Figure 139

**Step 2**: Click on a **Shape** from the drop list. Select the chart element and place or position shape on chart. Enter text, change size, color, etc.

Figure 140

**Step 3**: Drag the cursor to the position where you want to place the **Shape** on the chart. Select the enter button or right-click to apply the text box.

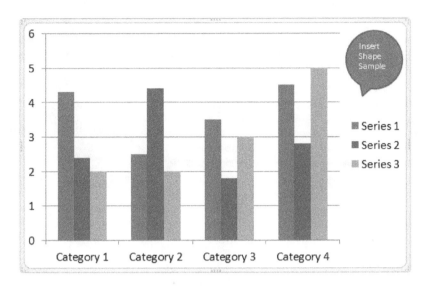

Figure 141

# Add a text box to a chart:

**Step 1**: Select **Text Box** icon from the **Insert** group on the **Layout** tab.

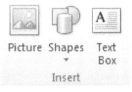

Figure 142

**Step 2**: Drag the cursor to the position where you want to place the text box. Draw the text box. Select the enter button or right-click to apply the text box.

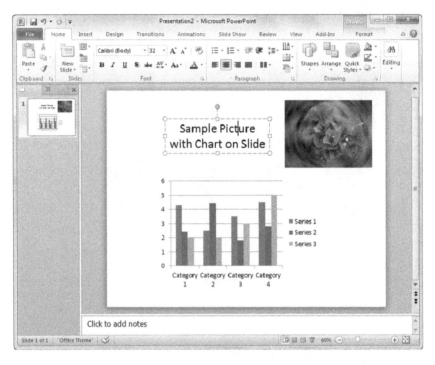

Figure 143

# Module 4:
# Practice Steps

## Interactive Practice Exercises:

**Step 1:** Create a **New Blank** presentation and insert **Movie** file from the **Clip Art Organizer.** Save the presentation as **"My New Movie Presentation."**

**Step 2:** Create a **New Blank** presentation. Insert a text list and convert it to a Smart Art graphic. Save as **"My New Smart Art".**

**Step 3**: Create a **New Blank** presentation. Insert a new table with 3 columns and two rows. Apply the table style **"Medium Style 2 - Accent 4".**

**Step 4:** Create a **New Blank** presentation. Insert a new table with 10 rows and 4 columns. Utilize the table and prepare your budget for 2012 and saved as **"My Budget for 2012".** Heading rows are Income, Expenses, Loans and Credit Cards and columns represent Jan, Feb, Mar, Apr, etc. for 2012.

**Step 5:** Open the **"My Budget for 2012"** presentation and change the **Credit Cards heading** to **Debt** and save.

**Step 6:** Create a **New Blank** presentation. Insert a photo from the Clip Art organizer. Save as **"My New Photo".**

**Step 7:** Open the **"My New Photo"** presentation and insert two new slides. One with a Photo Album and one with a Clip Art and saved as **"My New Combo Presentation".**

Module

5

# Easy Steps in Understanding Transitions and Animations

## OBJECTIVES

- Manage Built-in and Custom Animations
- Manage Effects and Path Options
- Manage Transitions between Slides
- Arrange Animations

## Understanding Transitions and Animations

This module will teach you the basics of animations and transitions of a slide presentation. You will understand how to step-by-step apply built-in and custom animations, effect and path options, work with transitions on slides, attach sound to animations, and manipulate animations.

## Manage Built-in and Custom Animations

This option will allow you to create built-in and custom animations.

## Apply an animation to a slide:

## Step 1: Select the **Animations** tab.

Figure 144

**Step 2**: You may apply animations to current slide or apply to all slides. Select one of the **Animation Effect** to the slide. Select the down arrow or the ⭐**Add Animation** icon.

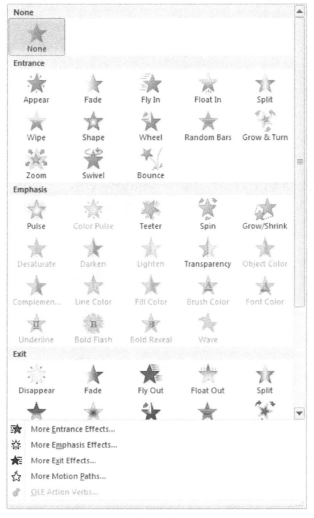

Figure 145

**Step 3**: Select a **None**, **Entrance**, **Exit** or **Emphasis** effect to apply to the slide.

## Animation pane:

**Step 1**: Click on **Animation Pane** icon from the **Advanced Animation** group on the **Animations** tab to display. You can modify or customized an animation from the animation pane.

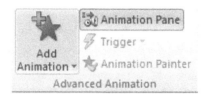

Figure 146

**Step 2**: The **Animation Pane** window will appear to the right of the slide. You can drag the **Animation Pane** window to position anywhere on the slide presentation.

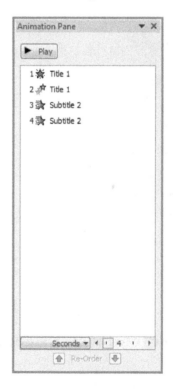

Figure 147

**Step 3**: Click the down arrow ▼ for more options of the **Animation Pane**. You can close, move, or size the **Animation Pane**.

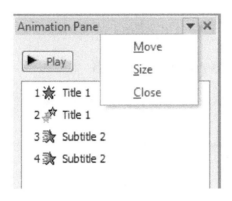

Figure 148

## Customize an animation on a slide:

**Step 1**: Click on **Animation Pane** icon from the **Advanced Animation** group on the **Animations** tab to display.

**Step 2**: Select the down arrow ▼ of the animation you want to customize.

**Step 3**: Select options from the drop down list to customize the selected animation.

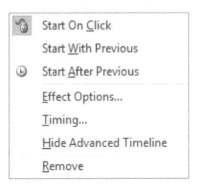

Figure 149

# Manage Effects and Path options

This option will allow you to create slide effects and path options.

### Add Animation effect options to slide:

**Step 1**: Select the **Animations** tab.

Figure 150

**Step 2**: Click on an existing animation on the slide or create a new animation.

**Step 3**: Select the **Effect Options** icon.

Figure 151

**Step 4**: Select a **Direction** or **Sequence** effect option. The changes will apply instantly to the animation.

Figure 152

## Add Path options to animations on a slide:

**Step 1**: Select the **Path Options from the Animations** tab. Click on the down arrow ⬇ to select from the **Motion Paths** section. You can also click ⭐ **Add Animation icon** and proceed with the following steps.

Figure 153

**Step 2**: Click on a **Motion Paths** option from the **Motion Paths** section. The changes will be applied instantly to the animation.

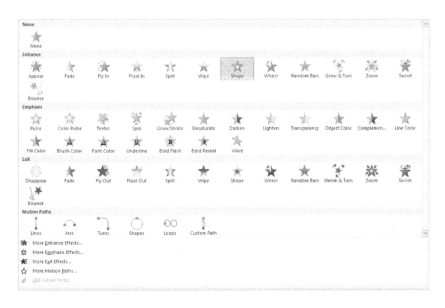

Figure 154

**Step 3**: Select **More Motion Paths** options for additional options.

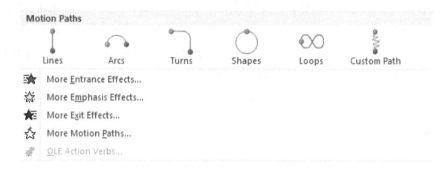

Figure 155

**Step 4:** Select a **Motion Path** option. Click on the **OK** button to apply changes.

Figure 156

## Manage transitions between slides.

The option will allow you to add or modify transitions; apply transition effect options, sound, and duration to slides.

## Add Transition to slide:

**Step 1**: Click on the slide you want to apply the transition. Select a **Transition** from the **Transitions** tab.

Figure 157

**Step 2**: The **Transition** selected will be applied to the slide.

### Add Transition effect options to slide:

**Step 1**: Select the **Transitions** tab.

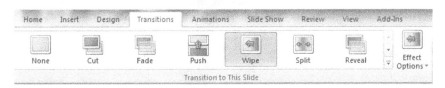

Figure 158

**Step 2**: Click on an existing **Transition** on the slide or create a new **Transition** from the **Transition to This Slide** group.

**Step 3**: Select the **Effect Options** icon.

Figure 159

**Step 4**: Select a **Transition** effect option from drop down list.

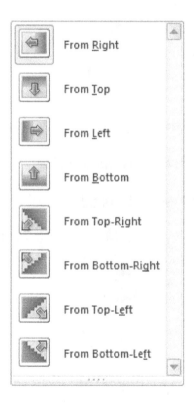

Figure 160

# Add Transition Sound to slide:

**Step 1**: Click on the slide you want to apply the Transition sound. Select the down arrow.

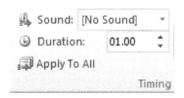

Figure 161

**Step 2**: A drop down selection of no sound and sound options will appear. Click on a sound option to apply to the slide. You can also select **Loop Until Next Sound** option

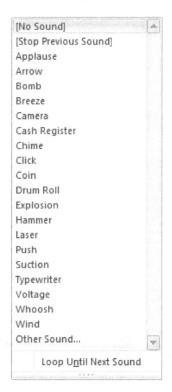

Figure 162

## Add Transition Duration to slide:

**Step 1**: Click on the slide you want to apply the **Transition Duration.** Select the down or up arrow for duration speed.

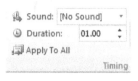

Figure 163

**Step 2**: The **Transition Duration** selected will be applied to the slide instantly.

TIP: You may select the **Apply To All** option for slides for apply **Transition Sound** or **Duration.**

## Arrange animations

You can modify, remove or reorder animations to a slide.

## Modify an animation on a slide:

**Step 1**: Click on the Animation to modify, select the down arrow ▼. Drop down list will appear with options.

**Step 2:** Select one of the options to make the change.

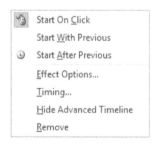

Figure 164

## Remove an animation on a slide:

**Step 1**: Click on the Animation to remove, select the down arrow 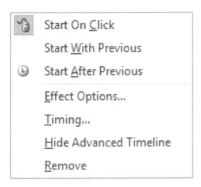. Drop down list will appear with options.

**Step 2:** Select the **Remove** option. The Animation will be removed from the **Animation** pane.

Figure 165

# Module 5:
# Practice Steps

## Interactive Practice Exercises

**Step 1:** Create a **New Blank** presentation. Add the title "Learning PowerPoint" and subtitle "**Add an Animation**". Add the **Fly In** animation, change the duration to **2 seconds (Medium)** and save as **"My New Animation"**.

**Step 2:** Open the "**My New Animation**" presentation from the previous step. Add the "**From the Top-Right**" effect option and save.

**Step 3**: Open the "**My New Animation**" presentation from the previous step. Add the **Wipe** animation. Change the duration to **5 seconds (Very slow)** and save.

**Step 4:** Open the "**My New Animation**" presentation from the previous step. Add another animation. Select the **Bounce** option and save.

**Step 5:** Open the "**My New Animation**" presentation from the previous step. Add the **Split** transition and save.

**Step 6:** Open the "**My New Animation**" presentation. Click on the **Animation pane.** Arrange or move the last animation to the first order of the presentation and save.

**Step 7:** Open the "**My New Animation**" presentation. Add the **Shapes** effects path option. Remove the **Bounce** animation.

Module

6

# Easy Steps in Understanding Collaboration on Presentations

## OBJECTIVES

- Manage Comments in Presentations
- Manage Proofing Tools

## Understanding Collaborations and Presentations

This module will teach you how manage comments and utilized proofing tools in presentations to assist you.

## Manage Comments in Presentations

This option will allow you to create, delete, and review comments in presentations.

## Add a new comment on a slide:

**Step 1:** Select the element on the slide you want to add comment.

**Step 2:** Select the **New Comment** icon from the **Comments** group.

Figure 166

**Step 3:** The **Comment** dialog box will appear. Enter comment. The author and date will automatically appear in the dialog box.

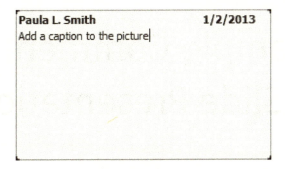

Figure 167

# Show Markup comment on a slide:

**Step 1:** Select the **Show Markup** icon from the **Comments** group on the **Review** tab.

Figure 168

**Step 2:** After **Show Markup** is selected, the comment will denote comment ID. (**For Example**: PLS2 in below figure)

# Sample Comments
# on Slide Presentations

Figure 169

## Edit a comment on a slide:

**Step 1:** Select the **Edit Comment** icon from the **Comments** group on the **Review** tab.

Figure 170

## Delete a comment on a slide:

**Step 1:** Select the **Delete** icon from the **Comments** group on the **Review** tab.

Figure 171

## Previous comment on a slide:

**Step 1:** Select the **Previous** icon from the **Comments** group on the **Review** tab.

Figure 172

## Next comment on a slide:

**Step 1:** Select the **Next** icon from the **Comments** group on the **Review** tab.

Figure 173

## Manage Proofing Tools

This option will allow you to check spelling, research, and utilized the thesaurus in proofing your presentations.

## Check Spelling in a Presentation:

**Step 1:** Highlight the text you want to check for correct spelling.

**Step 2:** Select the **Spelling** icon from the **Proofing** group on the **Review** tab.

Figure 174

## Apply the Research Tool in a Presentation:

This option will allow you to do research on words, etc., in the presentation slide show.

**Step 1:** Highlight the text you want to **Research** or type the text in the **Search For** dialog box.

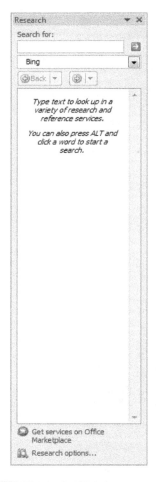

Figure 175

## Apply the Thesaurus Tool in a Presentation:

**Step 1:** Highlight the text you want the **Thesaurus** to find common words for or type the text in the **Search For** dialog box.

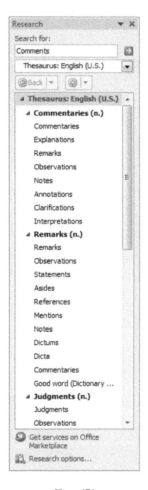

Figure 176

# Compare Presentations:

**Step 1:** Select the presentation you want to compare. **Click** the **Compare** icon from the **Review** tab.

Compare

Figure 177

**Step 2:** The **Choose File to Merge with Current Presentation** dialog box will appear.

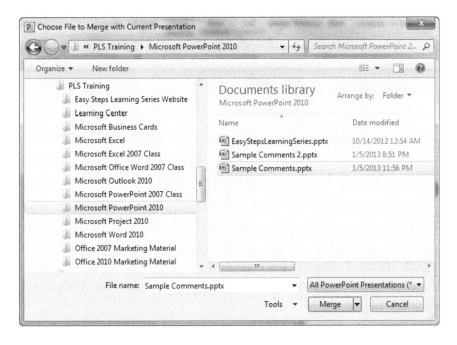

Figure 178

**Step 3:** Select the file to compare from documents library and select the **Merge** button.

**Step 4:** The **Revisions** pane will appear and show you the differences between the slide and show details.

Figure 179

**Step 5:** Select the **Reject** icon to reject changes when you merge or scroll through the changes using the **Reviewing Pane**.

Figure 180

# Module 6:
# Practice Steps

## Interactive Practice Exercises:

**Step 1**: Open a blank presentation. Create a title "**Learning PowerPoint**" and subtitle "**Working with Comments**". Insert a comment on the subtitle. Enter "**My first comment**" and Save As "**My Comments Presentation**".

**Step 2:** Open the presentation "**My Comments Presentation.**" Insert a comment. Enter "**My second comment**".

**Step 3:** Open the presentation "**My Comments Presentation**". Edit the second comment. Add the line "**Editing the second comment**".

**Step 4**: Open the presentation "**My Comments Presentation**". Insert a comment on the subtitle "**Working with Comments**". Enter "**My third comment**" and Check the Spelling throughout the presentation.

**Step 5:** Open the presentation "**My Comments Presentation**". Delete the "**My third comment**".

**Step 6:** Open the presentation "**My Comments Presentation**". Select the **Research** icon to find information on the definition of a comment and hide the **Comments** mark ups.

Module

7

# Easy Steps in Understanding Preparing Presentations for Delivery

## OBJECTIVES

- Manage Save Presentations
- Manage Sharing Presentations
- Manage Presentations File Types
- Manage Printing Presentations

# Understanding Preparing Presentations for Delivery

This module will teach you how to manage comments in presentations, proof presentations, share presentations, and save in various file types.

## Manage save presentations

This option will allow you to save in PowerPoint 2010 format or other file type formats.

**Step 1:** Select the **Save** or **Save As** option on the **File** Tab.

Figure 181

**Step 2:** Select a presentation **File Type** to save your file from the drop down list. After you select the file type, click the **Save As** button or click the **Save** button for standard 2010 file type (.pptx).

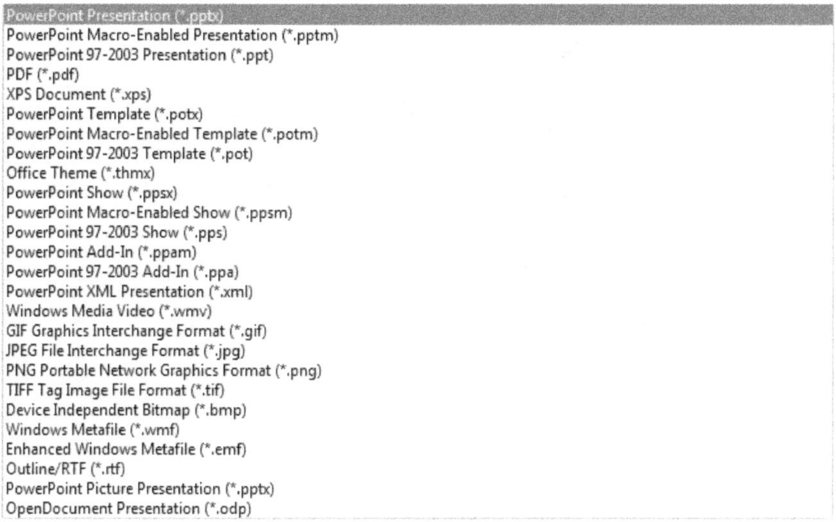

```
PowerPoint Presentation (*.pptx)
PowerPoint Macro-Enabled Presentation (*.pptm)
PowerPoint 97-2003 Presentation (*.ppt)
PDF (*.pdf)
XPS Document (*.xps)
PowerPoint Template (*.potx)
PowerPoint Macro-Enabled Template (*.potm)
PowerPoint 97-2003 Template (*.pot)
Office Theme (*.thmx)
PowerPoint Show (*.ppsx)
PowerPoint Macro-Enabled Show (*.ppsm)
PowerPoint 97-2003 Show (*.pps)
PowerPoint Add-In (*.ppam)
PowerPoint 97-2003 Add-In (*.ppa)
PowerPoint XML Presentation (*.xml)
Windows Media Video (*.wmv)
GIF Graphics Interchange Format (*.gif)
JPEG File Interchange Format (*.jpg)
PNG Portable Network Graphics Format (*.png)
TIFF Tag Image File Format (*.tif)
Device Independent Bitmap (*.bmp)
Windows Metafile (*.wmf)
Enhanced Windows Metafile (*.emf)
Outline/RTF (*.rtf)
PowerPoint Picture Presentation (*.pptx)
OpenDocument Presentation (*.odp)
```

Figure 182

# Manage sharing presentations

This option will allow you to share your presentation via email, web, SharePoint, broadcast or to a slide library.

## Send Presentation as an Email:

**Step 1**: Select the **Save and Send** option from the **File** tab.

**Step 2**: Click on **Send Using E-mail** option.

Figure 183

**Step 3:** Send the email in the following formats:

- Select the **Send as Attachment** icon to send as an attachment.

Send as Attachment

Figure 184

- Select the **Send a Link** icon to send as a link. It will only be enabled when the presentation is in a shared location.

Send a Link

Figure 185

- Select **Send as PDF** icon to send as a pdf document.

Figure 186

- Select the **Send as XPS** icon to send as an XPS document.

Send as XPS

Figure 187

- Select the **Send as Internet Fax** icon to send as an internet fax.

Send as
Internet Fax

Figure 188

## Save Presentation to the Web:

**Step 1**: Select the **Save and Send** option from the **File** tab.

**Step 2**: Click on **Send to Web** option.

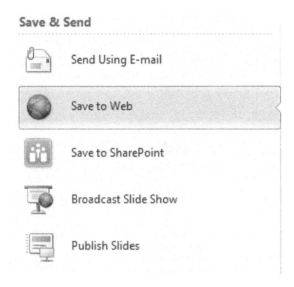

Figure 189

**Step 3:** Select the Windows **Sign In** icon to save to the web where others can access it.

Figure 190

# Save Presentation to SharePoint:

**Step 1**: Select the **Save and Send** option from the **File** tab.

**Step 2**: Click on **Save to SharePoint** option.

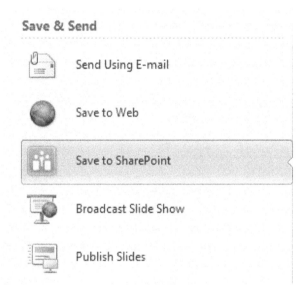

Figure 191

**Step 3:** Select the **Save As** icon to save to a SharePoint site to collaborate with others on the presentation.

Figure 192

## Broadcast a Slideshow:

**Step 1**: Select the **Save and Send** option from the **File** tab.

**Step 2**: Click on **Broadcast Slide Show** option.

Figure 193

**Step 3:** Select the **Broadcast Slide Show** icon to save to a web browser location to remote viewers.

Figure 194

**Step 4:** Select type **of Broadcast service options** and click on the **Start Broadcast button** to start.

Figure 195

## Publish Slides to a Slide Library:

**Step 1**: Select the **Save and Send** option from the **File** tab.

**Step 2**: Click on **Publish Slides** option.

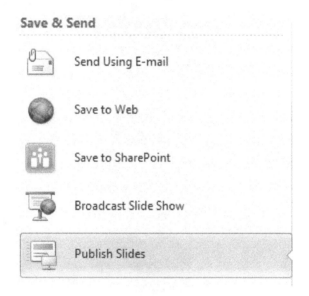

Figure 196

**Step 3**: Select the **Publish Slides icon.**

Figure 197

**Step 4:** The **Publish Slides dialog box** will appear.

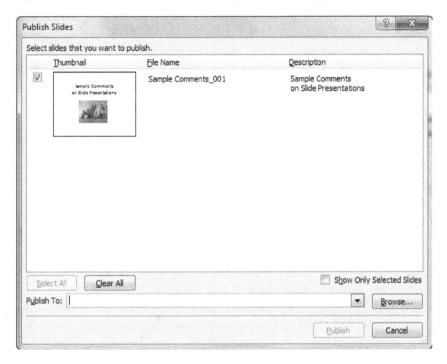

Figure 198

**Step 5:** Click on the **Browse** button and select the slides you want to publish.

**Step 6:** The **Select a Slide Library** dialog box will appear. Navigate to the location or folder to publish slides. Click the **Publish** button.

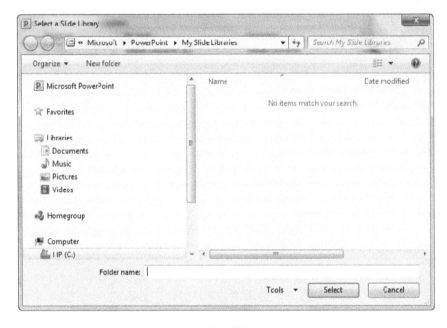

Figure 199

# Manage Presentations File Types

This option will allow you to save presentations in various media formats.

## Change File Types:

**Step 1**: Select the **Save and Send** option from the **File** tab.

**Step 2**: Click on **Change File Type** option.

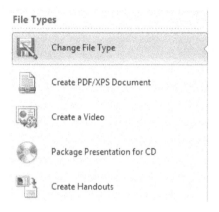

Figure 200

**Step 3:** Select a presentation file type from **Change File Type** dialog box.

**Step 4:** After you select the file type, click the **Save As** button. The file type selected will be defaulted. Click the **Save** button.

Figure 201

# Create PDF/XPS Document:

**Step 1**: Select the **Save and Send** option from the **File** tab.

**Step 2:** Select **Create PDF/XPS** icon to send as a pdf/xps document.

Figure 202

**Step 3:** The **Publish as PDF or XPS** dialog will appear. Select the **PDF** or **XPS** file type. Click on the **Publish** button to save.

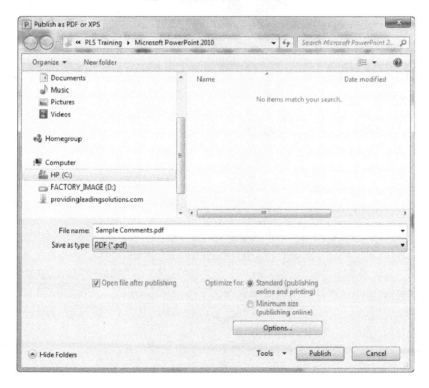

Figure 203

## Create a Video:

**Step 1**: Select the **Save and Send** option from the **File** tab.

**Step 2:** Select **Create Video** icon to create a video from the presentation.

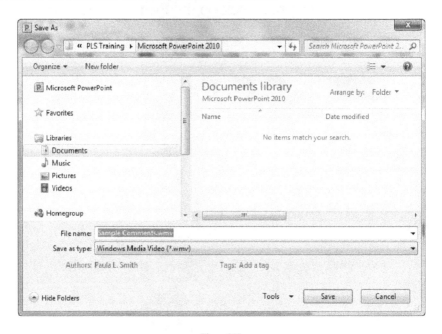

Figure 204

**Step 3:** The **Save As** dialog will appear. The media file type will be defaulted. Click the **Save** button.

Figure 205

## Package a Presentation for CD:

**Step 1**: Select the **Save and Send** option from the **File** tab.

**Step 2:** Select **Package for CD** icon to create media to be viewed on computers.

Figure 206

**Step 3:** The **Package for CD** dialog will appear. Select **Copy to Folder** or **Copy to CD**. Continue with next screen selections. Click the **Close** button when finished.

Figure 207

### Create Handouts:

**Step 1**: Select the **Save and Send** option from the **File** tab.

**Step 2:** Select **Create Handouts** icon to create handouts in word document format.

Figure 208

**Step 3:** The **Send to Microsoft Word** dialog box will appear. Select a page layout option for Microsoft Word format.

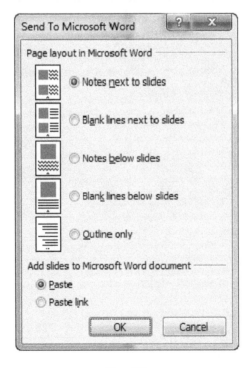

Figure 209

**Step 4:** Select the OK button to generate the handouts in Microsoft Word.

# Manage printing presentations

This option will allow you to print presentations.

**Step 1**: Select the **Save and Send** option from the **File** tab.

**Step 2:** Select **Print** option. Change the number of copies, printer, and settings. Click the **Print** button to print.

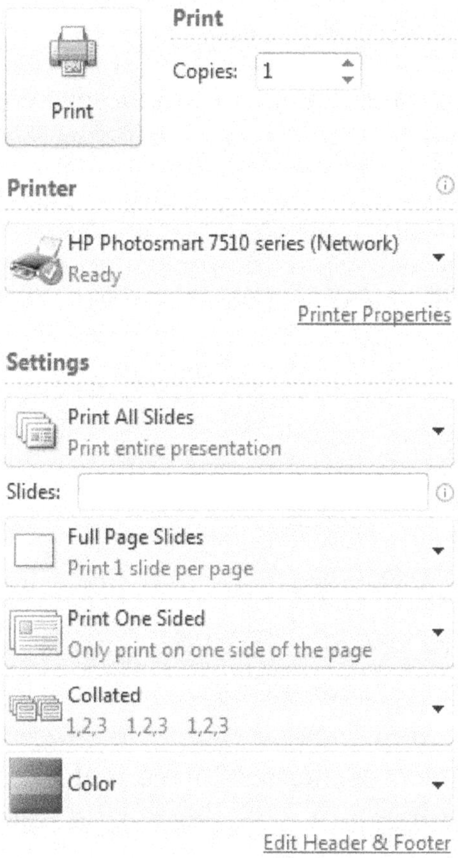

Figure 210

# Module 7:
# Practice Steps

## Interactive Practice Exercises:

**Step 1**: Create a presentation from the **Sample Templates** name "**Five Rules.**" Save the presentation. Save as five_rules.pdf document.

**Step 2:** Send the **five_rules.pdf** document via e-mail to you or a friend's e-mail account.

**Step 3:** Create a presentation from the **Sample Templates** name "**Quiz Show.**" Save the presentation as "**My Quiz Show**" and create handouts from the presentation.

**Step 4**: Open the presentation "**My Quiz Show**" and save as PowerPoint show.

**Step 5:** Open the presentation "**My Quiz Show**" and create a video.

**Step 6:** Open the presentation "**My Quiz Show**" and create a package presentation for a CD.

**Step 7:** Open the presentation "**Five Rules**" and save as Outline/RTF format.

**Step 8:** Print the "**Five Rules**" presentation in landscape orientation.

Module

8

# Easy Steps in Understanding Delivering Presentations

## OBJECTIVES

- Manage Presentations Tools
- Manage Setting up Slide Shows
- Manage Presentation Timing
- Manage Presentation Recording

## Understanding Delivering Presentations

This module will teach you how manage presentations tools, rehearse and time presentations, and record presentations.

## Manage presentations tools

This option will allow you to manage the presentations tools for the slide show.

## Navigating the Presentation:

**Step 1**: Select **From Beginning** or **From Current Slide** icons from the **Start Slide Show** group from the **Slide Show** tab. This will allow you start the presentation slide from the beginning or current slide.

From          From
Beginning  Current Slide

Figure 211

## Using more than one monitor during Presentation:

**Step 1**: Select the **Use Presenter View** box to enable to utilize two or more monitors.

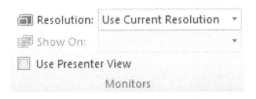

Figure 212

**Step 2:** The system will automatically check for multiple monitors. Select the **Check** button to verify or the **Cancel** button to exit.

Figure 213

**Step 3:** Select the down arrow to change to the resolution of the monitor or monitors in various aspect ratios.

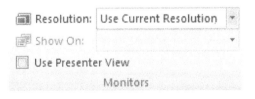

Figure 214

**Step 4:** Select from the drop down list or select the current resolution.

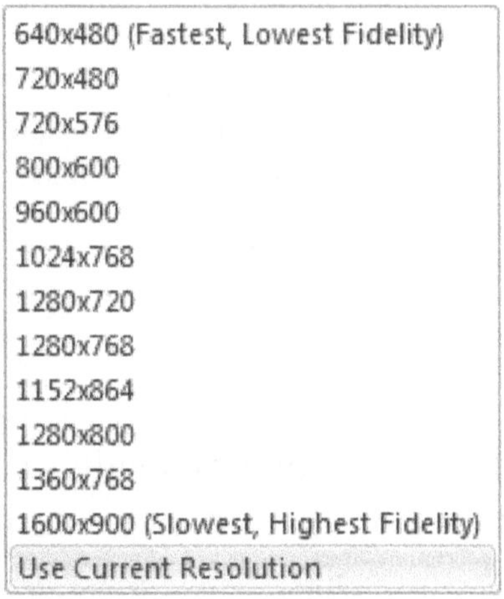

```
640x480 (Fastest, Lowest Fidelity)
720x480
720x576
800x600
960x600
1024x768
1280x720
1280x768
1152x864
1280x800
1360x768
1600x900 (Slowest, Highest Fidelity)
Use Current Resolution
```

Figure 215

# Manage setting up slide shows

This option will allow you to setup, customized or define a slide show.

# Set Up Slide Show:

**Step 1:** Select **Set Up Slide Show** icon from the **Set Up** group from the **Slide Show** tab.

Figure 216

**Step 2:** The **Set Up Slide Show** dialog box will appear. Change the show type, options, slides, advance slides, pen color, multiple monitors, etc. Click the **OK** button to apply changes.

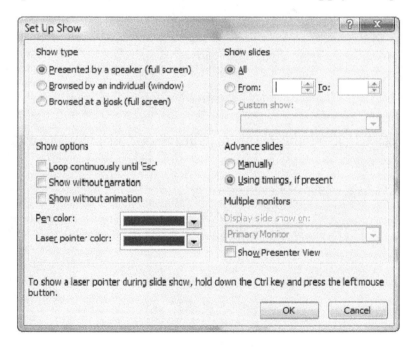

Figure 217

## Hide slide:

**Step 1:** Select **Hide Slide** icon to hide a slide from a slide show presentation.

Hide
Slide

Figure 218

## Customize your presentation:

**Step 1:** Select **Custom Slide Show** icon from the **Start Slide Show** group from the **Slide Show** tab.

Custom
Slide Show ▾

Figure 219

**Step 2:** Click on the **Custom Shows** option from drop down list.

Figure 220

**Step 3:** The **Custom Show**s dialog box will appear.

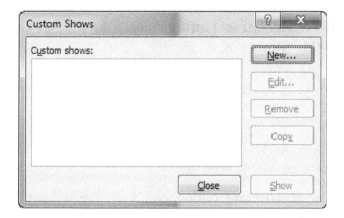

Figure 221

**Step 4:** Select the **New** option.

**Step 5:** The **Define Slide Show** dialog box will appear.

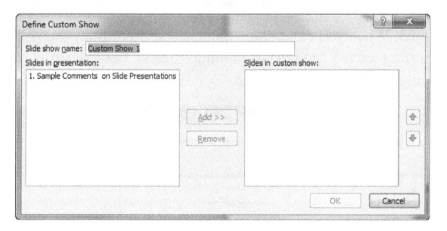

Figure 222

# Manage Presentation Timing

This option will allow you to set up and rehearse timings of your presentation.

## Rehearse your presentation:

**Step 1**: Select **Rehearse Timings** icon from the **Set Up** group from the **Slide Show** tab.

Rehearse
Timings

Figure 223

**Step 2**: The **Recording** dialog box will display and enter into rehearse record mode.

Figure 224

**Step 3**: When you exit or stop the rehearse recording, you will be prompted to keep rehearse timings. Select **Yes** to keep timings or **No** button to cancel.

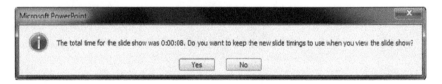

Figure 225

## Manage presentation recording

This option will allow you to set up and record your presentation.

## Set up recording of Presentation:

**Step 1**: Select **Record Slide Show** icon from the **Set Up** group from the **Slide Show** tab.

Record Slide
Show ▾

Figure 227

**Step 2**: Select **From Beginning** or **From Current Slide** from the drop down list. You can also select **Clear** option to reset recording.

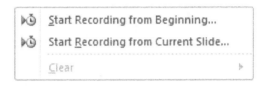

Figure 226

**Step 3**: The **Record Slide Show** dialog box will appear. Select the type of recording. Click the **Start Recording** button to start recording.

Figure 227

**Step 4**: The **Recording** dialog box will display and enter into record mode.

Figure 228

**Step 5**: When you exit or stop the recording, you will be prompted to keep recording timings. Select **Yes** to keep timings or **No** button to cancel.

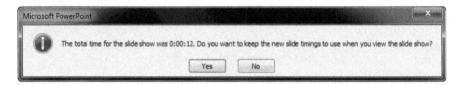

Figure 229

# Module 8:
# Practice Steps

## Interactive Practice Exercises:

**Step 1**: Create a presentation from the **Sample Templates** name "**Five Rules**". If the "**Five Rules**" presentation is already created from previous exercise in Module 7, open the presentation and view **From Beginning**.

**Step 2: O**pen the "**Five Rules**" presentation. Setup the slide show with the pen color of blue. Advance the slides manually.

**Step 3:** Rehearse the timing of the "**Five Rules**" presentation.

**Step 4**: Record the slide show of the "**Five Rules**" presentation.

**Step 5: O**pen the "**Five Rules**" presentation. Select the third slide and view **From Current Slide**.

**Step 6: O**pen the "**Five Rules**" presentation. Select the last slide. Hide the slide from presentation. View the slideshow From Beginning.

**Step 7: O**pen the "**Five Rules**" presentation. Setup the slide show with the laser pointer color green. Show the slide show without narration.

# Appendix I

## Review Questions

Instructions: Circle one of the multiple choice options below the question.

1) What do the Ribbon (UI) consist of?
   a) Menus, List and Check boxes
   b) Tabs, Groups and Group options
   c) Tabs, Messages and Reading panes

2) What command will allow you to open a new PowerPoint presentation?
   a) New
   b) Insert
   c) Presentation New

3) What keyboard command is the same as the "Copy" icon/button?
   a) CTRL + C
   b) CTRL + V
   c) CTRL + X

4) What keyboard command is the same as the "Cut" icon/button?
   a) CTRL + C
   b) CTRL + V
   c) CTRL + X

5) What keyboard command is the same as the "Paste" icon/button?
  a) CTRL + C
  b) CTRL + V
  c) CTRL + X

6) What command(s) will allow me to exit PowerPoint 2010?
  a) Exit
  b) Close
  c) Both A and B

7) What is the quickest way to start a PowerPoint 2010 slide show?
  a) View icon
  b) F5
  c) Slide Show icon

8) The backstage view will allow you to create presentations from templates, set permissions, save presentations in various file types, share presentations, create video, prepare package for CD, create handouts, and etc.?
  a) True
  b) False

9) What command would you use to start PowerPoint 2010?
  a) Start Button
  b) Run
  c) Control Panel

10) Which command is available in all 2010 Office programs and contain such commands as saving, opening, and printing.
   a) Run
   b) Microsoft Office® Button
   c) File

11) When might you use a Smart Art graphic?
   a) Whenever you have a bulleted list on a slide
   b) Whenever your information will have more impact, clarity, or usefulness if shown graphically
   c) Whenever you want to animate your points as you talk

12) When I change the color scheme of my PowerPoint environment, I must select Options on the File tab, click on General in the left panel and select from the Color Scheme drop down list to change settings?
   a) True
   b) False

13) What steps would I take to make the default language for PowerPoint in Spanish?
   a) Select General on the File tab, click on Language in the left panel, select from the Add Additional Editing language drop down list and Click the Add button
   b) Select Options on the Home tab, click on Language in the left panel, select from the Add Additional Editing language drop down list and Click the Add button
   c) Select Options on the File tab, click on Language in the left panel, select from the Add Additional Editing language drop down list and Click the Add button

14) In the PowerPoint window, what's the main area for adding slide content
   a) The Slides tab, where the slide thumbnails are, on the left of the window
   b) The notes pane
   c) The slide pane, in the middle of the window

15) When you apply a theme, it affects every slide in the presentation.
   a) True
   b) False

16) What command will allow you to save to another PowerPoint presentation format? (**For example: .pdf**)
   a) File Save
   b) Save As
   c) Save

17) What option lets me customized my presentation slide show?
   a) Set up Slide Show
   b) Custom Slide Show
   c) Custom Animation

18) How can I protect my presentation?
   a) Unrestricted Access option
   b) Read Access option
   c) Restricted Access option

19) What are some of the options you used to view your presentations?
   a) Slide Sorter
   b) Slide Show
   c) Slides Task Pane, Notes Page and Outline
   d) All of the Above

20) Which of these is not one of the main layout types within Smart Art graphics?
   a) Radial.
   b) Cycle.
   c) Matrix.

21) What command helps you minimize the impact of your photo's file size on the size of the presentation?
   a) Reset Picture
   b) Recolor
   c) Compress Pictures

22) You want to convert a bulleted list to a Smart Art graphic. What are the first steps?
   a) Click anywhere within the bulleted list to select it, and then click Convert to Smart Art Graphic on the Home tab
   b) Click the Insert tab, and click Smart Art Graphic within the Illustrations group
   c) Click anywhere within the bulleted list, and then click the Design tab

23) Which command will allow me to get Microsoft PowerPoint Help?
   a) F5
   b) F10
   c) F1

24) What steps do you take to create handouts from a presentation?
    a) Select the Save and Send option from the File tab, click the Create Handouts icon
    b) Select the Save and Send option from the Home tab, click the Create Handouts icon
    c) Select the Create Handouts option from the File tab, click the Publish Handouts icon

25) Is the Help command in every Microsoft Office® application?
    a) True
    b) False

26) Is the Ribbon (UI) located in every Microsoft Office® 2010?
    a) True
    b) False

27) Which option will allow for me to add a new comment to a presentation?
    a) Review
    b) Add Comment
    c) New Comment

28) Are you able to change the presentation theme?
    a) True
    b) False

29) On the Ribbon, where do you find the Rehearse timings option?
    a) Presentation tab
    b) Slide show tab
    c) Home tab

30) When I want to add a transition to a presentation, can I add additional effect options?
   a) True
   b) False

31) On the Ribbon, where do you find the Header or footer option for a presentation?
   a) Insert tab
   b) Slide show tab
   c) Presentation tab

32) What steps do you take to create a photo album presentation?
   a) Click the Photo Album icon from the Images group on the Insert tab
   b) Click the Image icon from the Images group on the Insert tab
   c) Click the Photo Album icon from the Pictures group on the Insert tab

33) When you create a presentation you can also broadcast the slide show?
   a) True
   b) False

34) On the Ribbon, where do you find the Text box option?
   a) Presentation tab
   b) Insert tab
   c) Home tab

35) When you create a presentation you can save as an XPS format?
   a) True
   b) False

36) On the Ribbon, where do you find the Master views of a presentation?
   a) Presentation tab
   b) Insert tab
   c) Home tab

37) When you create a presentation you can save as an XLS format?
   a) True
   b) False

38) What major command replaces the Microsoft Office® button in Microsoft Office® 2010 applications?
   a) Backstage View
   b) File Tab
   c) Office Tab

39) When you create a presentation you can create from an outline?
   a) True
   b) False

40) On the Ribbon, where do you find the Custom Slide show option?
   a) Review tab
   b) Custom tab
   c) Slide show tab

# Appendix II

## Review Answers

| | |
|---|---|
| 1. B | 26. A |
| 2. A | 27. C |
| 3. A | 28. A |
| 4. C | 29. B |
| 5. B | 30. A |
| 6. C | 31. A |
| 7. B | 32. A |
| 8. A | 33. A |
| 9. A | 34. B |
| 10. C | 35. A |
| 11. B | 36. C |
| 12. A | 37. A |
| 13. C | 38. B |
| 14. C | 39. A |
| 15. A | 40. C |
| 16. B | |
| 17. B | |
| 18. C | |
| 19. D | |
| 20. C | |
| 21. C | |
| 22. A | |
| 23. C | |
| 24. A | |
| 25. A | |

# Appendix III

## Bibliography

Gaskins, Robert. *Sweating Bullets: Notes about Inventing PowerPoint.* San Francisco and London: Vinland Books, 512 pp. 2012. http://www.robertgaskins.com/powerpoint-history/sweating-bullets/gaskins-sweating-bullets-webpdf-isbn-9780985142414.pdf/, accessed December 19, 2012.

Gaskins, Robert, *Resume of Robert Gaskins*. http://www.robertgaskins.com/, accessed December 19, 2012.

## Support and Feedback

Thank you for your support and feedback. We made every attempt to provide you with a simplistic step-by-step interactive technical book not full of inerrancy. We prepared the book with technical reviewers and numerous cycles of testing quality of the steps and processes performed throughout the modules.

If you need additional support or find any errors, please send an email message with page number and error description to Easy Steps Learning Series Support Team at:

errors@easystepslearningseries.com.

We appreciate any input or feedback about this book. Please send an email message to:

feedback@easystepslearningseries.com.